WORLD WAR II
EUROPE
CHRONICLE OF AMERICA'S WARS

Margaret J. Goldstein

LERNER PUBLICATIONS COMPANY
MINNEAPOLIS

Copyright © 2004 by Lerner Publications Company

Lerner Publications Company
A division of Lerner Publishing Group
241 First Avenue North
Minneapolis, MN 55401

Website address: www.lernerbooks.com

Library of Congress Cataloging-in-Publication Data

Goldstein, Margaret J.
    World War II—Europe / by Margaret J. Goldstein.
      p.   cm. — (Chronicle of America's wars)
    Summary: A chronicle of the United States and Allied forces' involvement in World War II Europe, including the political and social motivations for entering the war as well as major air, land, and sea campaigns. Includes bibliographical references and index.
      ISBN: 0–8225–0139–2 (lib. bdg. : alk. paper)
      1. World War, 1939–1945—Juvenile literature. [1. World War, 1939–1945.] I. Title: World War 2. II. Title: World War Two. III. Title. IV. Series.
    D743.7.G65 2004
    940.53—dc22   2003012846

Manufactured in the United States of America
1 2 3 4 5 6 – JR – 09 08 07 06 05 04

Table of Contents

INTRODUCTION

It was daybreak on June 6, 1944. Private Bruce Bradley, a twenty-four-year-old U.S. Army radio operator, was about to join one of the most famous assaults in military history—D-Day, the invasion of Normandy, France, in World War II.

Bradley waited on a naval ship, preparing to climb down a rope ladder into a landing craft that would ferry him and other soldiers to Utah Beach. He recalled, "The sea was rough and it was dark. The navy guys had remarked that they were glad they were in the navy at this point. I'm sure they were. We got *V* for Victory signs from them as they helped us over the side. Victory didn't seem possible at the time, to me. Survival, maybe."

Private Bradley was one of millions of men and women who fought in World War II, a war that lasted for six years, from 1939 to 1945. The fighting took place in two main areas—in Europe and on the islands and seas of the Pacific Ocean. D-Day marked a turning point in the war in Europe. With the invasion of Normandy, the United States and its allies began a massive ground war against the German enemy, which had conquered most of Europe only several years earlier.

Bradley remembered approaching the beach in the landing craft: "Making the run to shore, the sky was intermittently lit by explosions, some of them of tremendous force. Bombs, shells from the battleships standing out to sea, rockets whooshing overhead, ack-ack from German positions, and tracers were coming and going. An awesome display."

Then Bradley heard a deafening blast. "We were thrown down or knocked sideways. We had been hit by a shell. The coxswain was gone, the ramp was down, the boat was sinking. Sideways," he explained. "Most guys in that boat drowned. . . . I dog-paddled toward the shore until my feet found sand."

Bruce Bradley survived that watery nightmare and the year of deadly fighting that followed. But he never bragged. He did his duty, risked death, and returned home to the United States. In this, Bradley was like many others. During World War II, the United States created the greatest military machine the world has ever known. They fought on battlegrounds in Europe and the Pacific. Then they went home and carried on with their lives. But their heroic actions will never be forgotten. And their stories deserve retelling. This book tells the story of World War II in Europe, and the U.S. soldiers who fought there.

MILITARY SPEAK: D-DAY
People disagree about when the term *D-Day* was first used and what it stands for. But U.S. military documents suggest that this term for the first day of a mission has been used in military planning for some time, when that day is not set or is secret.

FAST FACT

THE FORECAST
CALLS FOR WAR

A world war doesn't start without reasons. World War II had its roots in World War I, which raged in Europe from September 1914 to November 1918. World War I pitted the Central powers, led by Germany and Austria-Hungary, against the Allied powers, led by France, Great Britain, and the United States. The war ended with an Allied victory. The Treaty of Versailles, which officially ended the war, changed borders all across Europe. The treaty broke up the Austro-Hungarian and German Empires, created new nations, and gave other nations additional territory.

Bitterness from these changes ran deep. Millions of people ended up living within new national borders, governed by people of a different ethnic group. For instance, many former German citizens found themselves living in Poland, Czechoslovakia, Austria, Denmark, Belgium, or France. These Germans, torn without their consent from their homeland, were called Ausland Deutsch ("outsider Germans").

FAST FACT

THE GERMAN ECONOMIC CRASH

The German mark (unit of money) fell in value during and after World War I. By 1923 the mark was worthless. It took millions of marks to buy goods. The German people were thrown into poverty and were desperate for new leaders who might help them.

ECONOMIC HARDSHIP

The Great Depression started in 1929. All around the globe, businesses failed and banks closed. Unemployment and homelessness skyrocketed. In Germany the economy utterly collapsed. Some Germans froze or starved to death because they couldn't afford fuel or food. The German people needed new leaders who could solve their problems.

Adolf Hitler appeared to be that kind of leader. He founded the Nazi (National Socialist) Party in Germany in the 1920s. Hitler glorified German culture, promised to restore the German economy, and blamed minority groups for all of Germany's problems. His message appealed to many German voters. By late 1932, the Nazis had won the largest block of seats in the Reichstag, the German parliament. General Paul von Hindenburg, the elected president of Germany, named Hitler chancellor, or prime minister (the chief government executive), on January 30, 1933.

As chancellor, Hitler began to undermine the regular German police. He created a separate police force, made up of his most loyal and enthusiastic Nazi Party members. One of Hitler's friends, Hermann Goering, created a reserve police force of 50,000 Nazi Party fanatics. Few Germans objected to more police. They thought Hitler's police force would help make Germany safer.

On February 27, 1933, the Reichstag building was set on fire. Hitler blamed the Communist Party, a political group with ties to the Soviet Union. The following day, the German government issued an

Chancellor Adolf Hitler *(left center)*, President Paul Ludwig von Hindenburg *(center)*, and other members of the German government in 1933. Hindenburg did not agree with Hitler's ideas and politics, but public pressure and Nazi control of the German parliament forced him to name Hitler to power.

emergency order suspending people's constitutional rights. The government claimed the order was necessary to help the police protect people from Communists. Hindenburg called another election, and the Nazis won a majority of seats in the Reichstag. On March 23, 1933, the Reichstag granted Hitler unlimited power for four years. Hitler had become a dictator, but every step he had taken to achieve that position had been perfectly legal.

NAZI DICTATORSHIP

Hitler used his control of the police to eliminate opposition. He outlawed, disbanded, or took over all non-Nazi political parties and Catholic organizations. He seized the funds and property of trade unions. His police force arrested intellectuals, priests, socialists, homosexuals, the handicapped, and ethnic minorities such as Gypsies, Russians, and Jews. Other Germans had no idea that those arrested by the police were not going to get a fair trial. Instead, Hitler's victims were sent directly to prison camps.

Hitler claimed that German Christians—particularly those with fair skin, light hair, and blue eyes—belonged to a superior race, which he called Aryan. He used this idea to justify persecution of Jews and other minority groups. He forced Jews out of government jobs, seized their property, and restricted their travel. Many Germans blamed the Jews in part for Germany's defeat in World War I, so they didn't object to Hitler's policies.

Dictator Adolf Hitler *(standing in car)* **and the head of the German elite forces (SS), Heinrich Himmler** *(standing next to car),* **inspect SS troops** *(marching at left).* **Himmler's SS provided the muscle necessary to control German opponents to Hitler and to assure he stayed in power.**

By July 14, 1933, the Nazi Party was the only legal party in Germany. Hindenburg died of natural causes in 1934, and Hitler became president. He created a new soldier's oath. Previously, German soldiers had sworn loyalty to the German government and constitution. Under the new oath, soldiers swore to obey Hitler personally.

In 1935 Hitler declared that Jews were no longer German citizens. He forced Jews to wear identification badges: yellow stars sewn onto their clothing. Homosexuals were identified by pink triangles. Most Germans didn't oppose Hitler's actions, because he had also begun a series of programs to put Germans back to work. In the wake of the Depression, his economic efforts were popular.

On March 16, 1935, Hitler denounced the Treaty of Versailles. He started a military buildup and secretly told his generals to prepare for war. In March 1936, Hitler broke the treaty, sending troops into the demilitarized Rhineland (region of western Germany bordering France, Belgium, and the Netherlands). World governments did little in response.

BLITZKRIEG

The Germans wanted to assure their victory in a new war. Brainstorming ideas with other officers, Major Heinz Guderian created a new form of warfare, called blitzkrieg (lightning war). Guderian's ideas took advantage of new technology, especially new tanks called *panzerkampfwagens,* or panzers. Panzers were faster and better armed than the tanks used during World War I. During a

> **EYEWITNESS QUOTE: ON WAGING WAR**
>
> "In starting and waging a war, it is not right that matters but victory."
>
> —Adolf Hitler

blitzkrieg, tanks—along with infantry (foot soldiers) and artillery (large firearms)— would break through enemy lines and sweep into the rear. Once there, they would destroy the enemy's artillery, reinforcements, and head- quarters and then destroy the leaderless and unsupported soldiers.

The Germans also created a new type of air force. They developed planes specifically for fighting—shooting down enemy air- planes—and dive-bombing, or precise bombing at very low altitude. They organized this air force, called the Luftwaffe (air weapon), to support blitzkrieg. Hitler appointed Goering to command the Luft- waffe. By the late 1930s, Germany had com- pleted work on its new tanks, planes, and tactics. Using speed on the ground and destruction from the air, all coordinated by radio, the Germans would surprise the world.

THE AXIS POWERS DECLARE WAR

War was brewing in other parts of the world too. In 1922 Benito Mussolini had come to power in Italy. Mussolini promised to restore Italy to world leadership and started a military buildup in Africa in the Italian colonies of Somaliland, Eritrea, and Libya. In the 1930s, Mussolini threatened Albania, to Italy's east, and the East African nation of Ethiopia. No other nation objected. After accusing Ethiopia of a border violation against Eritrea, Mussolini invaded Ethiopia in October 1935. The Italian air force bombed defenseless Ethiopian villages. Despite personal pleas from Emperor Haile Selassie of Ethiopia, the rest of the world did nothing.

Hitler's Third Reich

Hitler called his regime the Third Reich, or third empire. Hitler's Third Reich followed two earlier German empires. Friedrich Barbarossa led the first during the 1100s, and the second flourished from the 1860s to World War I (1914–1918).

Also in the 1930s, in the Far East, Japan invaded China. No nation moved to stop Japan either. Adolf Hitler signed pacts with both Italy and Japan. These three invading nations became known as the Axis powers.

In March 1938, Hitler's troops occupied Austria. He forced both German and Austrian Jews into squalid, cramped ghettos. In September Hitler prepared to seize the Sudetenland (the Ausland Deutsch areas of Czechoslovakia). Czechoslovakia mobilized for war. It asked for help from other nations. But those nations, including France and Britain, decided not to help. The Czechs submitted and gave Hitler the Sudetenland.

In March 1939, Hitler seized another large portion of Czechoslovakia. Once again, the rest of the world watched but did nothing.

Hitler pressured Poland to give Germany its Ausland Deutsch territory. Poland refused and prepared for war. On August 23, 1939, Hitler secretly signed a nonaggression pact with Joseph Stalin, the brutal Communist dictator of the Soviet Union. Hitler and Stalin agreed not to fight each other and to divide Poland and other conquered nations between them.

At 4:45 A.M. on September 1, 1939, Germany attacked Poland. Poland appealed to other nations for help. Britain and France finally decided that Hitler had gone too far and declared war on Germany. British colonies and former colonies, including India, Australia, New Zealand, Rhodesia (modern-day Zimbabwe), South Africa, and Canada followed suit. As in World War I, the nations fighting against Germany were known as the Allies. World War II had begun.

A German panzer division receives recognition for its role in Germany's capture of Poland in 1939.

THE GERMAN POINT OF VIEW

To many Germans, Hitler and the Nazi Party represented hope for the future in the face of a difficult present. On the heels of the Depression, Hitler brought economic recovery and then prosperity to Germany. His government built the autobahn, a highway system that greatly improved transportation. The government also built electrical generation plants and wiring networks that brought electricity to nearly every German household. Hitler's economic policies restored the value of German money and stabilized the nation's banking system. For the first time in two decades, a German citizen could afford to buy a house and raise a family.

German citizens and members of the Nazi Party cheer for and salute Hitler in the 1930s.

Hitler and the Nazi Party also went to great lengths to glorify German culture. The Nazis promoted art and music. At some factories, orchestras played music for workers during lunch hour. To many Germans, the economic and cultural improvements were signs that Germany was far better off with Hitler.

Propaganda is a method of spreading information, ideas, or even rumors that support a cause or undermine an opposing cause. Hitler created an effective propaganda machine designed to promote Nazi ideals and programs. Headed by Joseph Goebbels, the Propaganda Ministry used both print and radio to publicize economic success stories and cultural messages. Hitler also used impressive rallies—featuring parades of uniformed soldiers, impassioned speeches, and rousing music—to stir the German people. The Nazi symbol, the swastika (a cross with bent arms), was displayed extensively. Slowly but surely, the average German began to believe that Hitler was the best leader for Germany.

Hitler justified the start of the war in terms of righting the wrongs of World War I, bringing the Ausland Deutsch back into Germany, and defending the nation against foreign attack. He especially played on people's fears of Communism and Joseph Stalin's brutal Communist regime in the Soviet Union. As the war worsened for Germany, the government tried to keep up morale. It rarely mentioned German defeats in news broadcasts. It continued to play on German fears of Communism. It also praised the strong resistance of the German people in the face of Allied attacks.

2) SWASTIKA ON THE MARCH

Hitler had planned the attack on Poland well. First, the Luftwaffe struck Polish airfields and destroyed most of the Polish air force on the ground. Then the Luftwaffe supported blitzkrieg. Two German army groups attacked toward Warsaw, the Polish capital, from different directions. If these attacks succeeded, the Polish armies would be surrounded. They would have to surrender or die.

In three days, German units advanced 40 miles into Poland. The Polish army fought hard but was doomed. The Poles tried to withdraw, but before they could regroup, the Germans got behind them and encircled them. Heinz Guderian's XIX Panzer Corps charged 100 miles to the east, then swung south along the Bug River, preventing escape. One by one, the encircled Poles surrendered. Stalin's armies, in keeping with the nonaggression pact, occupied all of Poland east of the Bug River.

WAR IN THE BALTIC

As part of the nonaggression pact, Hitler agreed to let Stalin take over the nations of Lithuania, Latvia, Estonia, and Finland, located on the Baltic Sea. Stalin easily took the first three, but the Finns fought back. They hung on for four months before negotiating for peace in March 1940. Meanwhile, Hitler made plans to attack France and Britain. First, he wanted to conquer the northern nations of Denmark and Norway. This conquest would secure his northern flank (side), and the captured seaports in Norway would help his navy fight the British.

The German invasion struck on April 9, 1940. Denmark offered no resistance to the attack. The Norwegian army fought bravely, however. Britain and France sent reinforcements, but their planes couldn't cover the distance to Norway, so they couldn't stop the Luftwaffe. They withdrew on May 3. The Norwegians surrendered on May 5.

THE INVASION OF FRANCE

Hitler's next targets were Belgium, the Netherlands, and France. The Belgians and Netherlanders (also called Dutch) had declared themselves neutral. British troops, who had arrived to help the French, were posted along the French-Belgian border. They couldn't take positions in Belgium because of Belgian neutrality.

Hitler didn't care that Belgium and the Netherlands had declared neutrality. He planned to attack them anyway. At the same time, German general Karl Rudolph

Hitler's War against the Jews

As early as 1934, Hitler began to rid Germany of people he disapproved of: Jews, Catholics, Communists, homosexuals, Gypsies, and others he regarded as "racially inferior" or politically dangerous. The "unfit" were systematically removed from government, education, and business through legal and questionable means. Many were arrested and sent to prison camps.

Anti-Jewish actions became harsher, erupting in violence toward German Jews and destruction of their property during Kristallnacht (Night of Broken Glass) in November 1938. Ultimately, the Nazi-controlled Reichstag declared that Jews were noncitizens and enemies of the Third Reich. The Nazi government sent all German and Austrian Jews to prison camps or isolated ghettos.

As the German military advanced through Europe in 1939 and the early 1940s, the Nazi government imposed its policies on conquered nations. Prison camps and ghettos were set up. Jews and other groups were rounded up and sent to those ghettos and camps.

A woman turns away from the gate of the Lodz Ghetto in Lodz, Poland. Within months of the capture of Lodz in 1939, the Nazis established this early ghetto, separating Jewish citizens from other Poles. The city's Jewish citizens, more than 230,000, were ordered to stay within or move to the ghetto in early 1940.

Gerd von Rundstedt's armies would invade France at one lightly defended place: the Ardennes Forest. The Ardennes lay between the French and British forces. Both the French and British believed that the dense stands of trees there would serve as barriers to panzers.

On May 10, 1940, the Germans attacked. The Dutch collapsed. Rundstedt's infantry quickly cleared the Ardennes of defenders. His 7th Panzer Division, commanded by Erwin Rommel, emerged from the Ardennes and charged into the rear of the British troops facing Belgium.

Rundstedt's armies quickly pushed across France to the English Channel, which separates France and Britain. By June 24, Rundstedt had trapped 380,000 Allied troops (mostly British) at the French coastal town of Dunkirk. Hitler ordered the Luftwaffe to destroy the troops at Dunkirk and Rundstedt to attack the south of France.

But the Luftwaffe wasn't up to the job. British fighter planes battled the Luftwaffe to a standstill. Then British naval vessels, joined by British civilians in private yachts and other boats, set out to rescue their trapped soldiers. By June 5, when Dunkirk

Under heavy attack from the Luftwaffe, British soldiers leave the port town of Dunkirk, France, in 1940. Over a period of eight days in May and June, 848 private and military boats and ships carried some 338,000 troops out of Dunkirk to the safety of Great Britain in an evacuation known as Operation Dynamo.

A victorious Adolf Hitler *(center)* stands before the Eiffel Tower in Paris, France, in June 1940. The photograph was taken during Hitler's tour of triumph through the French capital city. The men with Hitler are Minister of Armaments (weapons) Albert Speer *(left)* and Nazi Party sculptor Arno Becker *(right)*.

fell to the Germans, more than 338,000 soldiers had been evacuated across the English Channel back to England.

While the British evacuated Dunkirk, Rundstedt reorganized, faced south, and attacked. Guderian's panzers broke through at Châlons-sur-Marne, France, and swept into the French rear. With his armies disintegrating, Marshal Philippe Pétain of France asked the Germans for a cease-fire, which was signed on June 22. Hitler occupied the north of France with German soldiers. He left Pétain to govern the south of France. Pétain's government, based in the city of Vichy, was actually a "puppet" government—largely under German control.

Many French citizens refused to show loyalty to either the Germans in the north or Pétain in the south, however. A group of resistance fighters called the French Forces of the Interior continued to fight the Germans within France. At the same time, French general Charles de Gaulle fled to London. There he organized a government in exile called the Free French, complete with a trained and equipped army. De Gaulle's government joined the Allies.

Saint Paul's Cathedral in London, England, is hit in a German bombing raid during the Battle of Britain in 1940. A symbol of British history, culture, and strength, the great church, though damaged, remained standing.

THE BATTLE OF BRITAIN

Next, Hitler wanted to invade Great Britain, but he had to take control of British airspace to do so. Starting on July 10, German planes attacked Great Britain in what became known as the Battle of Britain. But the German planes were designed to support blitzkrieg, not an extended bombing campaign unsupported by ground forces. Goering, head of the Luftwaffe, was a poor decision maker. Sometimes he bombed London, an action that killed civilians and enraged the British people. Then he attacked factories, ports, airfields, or radar stations. But he never selected a vital target and kept bombing until he destroyed it. That allowed the British to hang on and keep shooting down German aircraft. On October 31, after losing more than 2,000 planes, Goering stopped the attacks.

As the Battle of Britain raged, Hitler sent troops into Hungary, just east of Austria, and Romania, farther east on the Balkan Peninsula. Bulgaria, another Balkan nation, saw resisting Hitler's blitzkrieg was useless and secretly allied itself with the Nazi government.

> ### EYEWITNESS QUOTE: BATTLE OF BRITAIN
>
> "We shall fight on the beaches. We shall fight on the landing grounds. We shall fight in the fields, and in the streets, we shall fight in the hills. We shall never surrender."
>
> —Prime Minister Winston Churchill, address to the British House of Commons, 1940

MUSSOLINI MAKES A MESS

Benito Mussolini was also on the offensive. His troops in Libya attacked east into Egypt on September 13. The Italians tried to capture the British-held Suez Canal, a vital waterway linking the Mediterranean Sea with the Red Sea, but British troops stopped them in three days.

On October 28, Italian troops in Albania invaded Greece to the south. Though the Italians looked superior on paper (the Greeks had no tanks), the Greeks stopped Mussolini's soldiers. When the British Royal Air Force arrived to help on November 3, the Greeks counterattacked. By November 18, Greek forces had entered Albania.

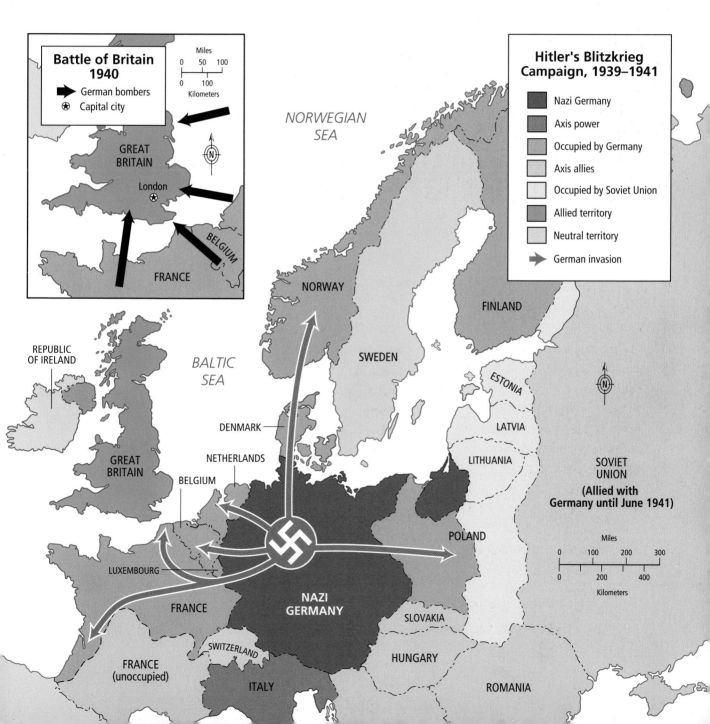

Battle of Britain 1940

→ German bombers
✪ Capital city

Miles
0 50 100

Kilometers
0 100

GREAT BRITAIN

London ✪

BELGIUM

FRANCE

Hitler's Blitzkrieg Campaign, 1939–1941

Nazi Germany
Axis power
Occupied by Germany
Axis allies
Occupied by Soviet Union
Allied territory
Neutral territory
→ German invasion

NORWEGIAN SEA

NORWAY

FINLAND

REPUBLIC OF IRELAND

BALTIC SEA

SWEDEN

ESTONIA

LATVIA

DENMARK

NETHERLANDS

LITHUANIA

SOVIET UNION
(Allied with Germany until June 1941)

GREAT BRITAIN

BELGIUM

POLAND

LUXEMBOURG

NAZI GERMANY

Miles
0 100 200 300

Kilometers
0 200 400

FRANCE

SLOVAKIA

SWITZERLAND

HUNGARY

FRANCE (unoccupied)

ITALY

ROMANIA

General Erwin Rommel of the Afrika Korps *(standing front)* looks out over the Libyan desert in 1941. Called the Desert Fox, Rommel and his 15th Panzer Division won battle after battle that year.

On December 9, 1940, the British counterattacked the Italians in Egypt. By February 5, 1941, the British had crossed half of Libya and destroyed or captured nearly all the Italian forces there. Hitler couldn't let the Italians lose North Africa to the British. So he created the Afrika Korps and promoted Erwin Rommel to command it. Rommel moved the Afrika Korps to Libya. He entered Egypt on April 14. Then he ran out of supplies and had to stop.

On April 6, 1941, the Germans attacked Yugoslavia and Greece. With a year and a half of experience in planning and executing complex military operations, the Germans crushed Yugoslavia in just 11 days. Greece lasted only slightly longer. The Greek soldiers and British reinforcements didn't work well together. German troops overwhelmed them, breaking through to their rear and forcing them to retreat. Athens, the capital of Greece, fell on April 27. By April 30, the British forces had evacuated, and the Greeks had surrendered.

Despite Mussolini's blunders, Hitler had won the advantage in the Mediterranean region. He failed to complete his victory, however. He didn't have the Luftwaffe sweep the British Royal Navy from the Mediterranean Sea. He didn't have Rommel take the Suez Canal. Instead, Hitler moved almost all his forces to the border with the Soviet Union.

THE PRICE OF GERMAN SUCCESS

Germany had been on an incredible roll of success. But success can sometimes breed failure. Mindful of the economic suffering that had helped him gain power, Hitler did not fully convert German industry to wartime production. Instead of making as many weapons and other military supplies as possible, German factories kept producing civilian goods such as cars and washing machines. Hitler wanted to keep making consumer goods to keep the German people happy and to maintain public support.

But Hitler did not realize that his string of victories had awakened a sleeping giant. Although the United States was at peace, its army and navy were planning for war. U.S. industrial engineers were working at a feverish pace, converting U.S. industries for war production.

Hitler and the Jews: The United States Drags Its Feet

In the United States, most citizens were unaware of Hitler's persecution of European Jews. Gradually, however, stories of the ghettos, prison camps, and killings began to reach U.S. leaders, including President Franklin D. Roosevelt. Many people in the United States, either because of anti-Semitic (anti-Jewish) attitudes or a desire to stay out of the European war, chose to ignore the situation. But the Jewish community in the United States pressured the U.S. government to allow more Jewish refugees into the United States. The Roosevelt administration was slow to respond.

The U.S. policy proved tragic. For example, on May 27, 1939, a passenger ship named the *St. Louis,* carrying 900 German Jewish refugees, arrived in Havana, Cuba. Cuba had previously provided a safe haven for European Jews. But the Cuban government had changed its policy and would not admit the refugees. The U.S. government refused to help, arguing that the situation was a Cuban matter. With nowhere to go, the *St. Louis* had to head back to Germany. In June Great Britain, the Netherlands, France, and Belgium intervened, agreeing to admit the ship's passengers themselves. But Germany soon overran three of these nations and eventually killed most of the Jews there, including most of the *St. Louis* passengers.

Following months of protests, the Roosevelt administration held several meetings regarding Hitler's treatment of Jews soon after the United States entered the war in 1941. The administration condemned the killings but took no concrete steps to either rescue Jews from prison camps or to increase the number of Jews allowed to seek protection in the United States. Finally, in early 1944, Roosevelt created the War Refugee Board, which enabled more Jewish refugees to enter the United States and other neutral countries. But by then, millions of Jews had already been killed.

THE GREAT
PATRIOTIC WAR

3

On June 22, 1941, despite the nonaggression pact signed earlier, Hitler invaded the Soviet Union in an attack called Operation Barbarossa. He thought the Soviets were inferior fighters and believed they would fall in three months. The Germans attacked with three army groups—North, South, and Center—and four panzer groups. The panzers were supposed to penetrate the Soviet lines and get deep into the rear. Once there, they would link up to encircle the Soviet armies, much as they'd done in Poland.

The plan worked. In less than 10 days, the Germans encircled the Soviets at the city of Minsk and captured 290,000 soldiers. On July 19, the Germans did it again at Smolensk. In the Center group, German armies covered two-thirds of the distance to Moscow, the Soviet capital. The campaign looked very successful.

Then Hitler changed his mind, interrupting the campaign. He removed the panzer groups from Army Group Center, sending one each to Army Groups North and South. He changed his objective, or goal, from Moscow in the center to the northern city of Leningrad, named after Communist hero Vladimir Lenin, and to a mountainous region called the Caucasus. Hitler wanted to demoralize the Soviets by capturing a city named after their hero. He wanted the Caucasus so he could use the oil from its oil fields to make gasoline.

In the south, Guderian's 2nd Panzer Group, acting together with Rundstedt's forces, encircled the city of Kiev. On September 26, about 665,000 Soviet soldiers surrendered in Kiev. Then Hitler changed his mind again. He sent Guderian back to Army Group Center. Guderian and his troops traveled more than 400 miles, then helped encircle another 658,000 Soviets at Bryansk.

Hitler's repeated changes of mind wasted time. Stalin used the delay to sign a neutrality pact with Japan, assuring peace on his eastern border. That allowed him to move troops from the east to face the Germans in the west instead.

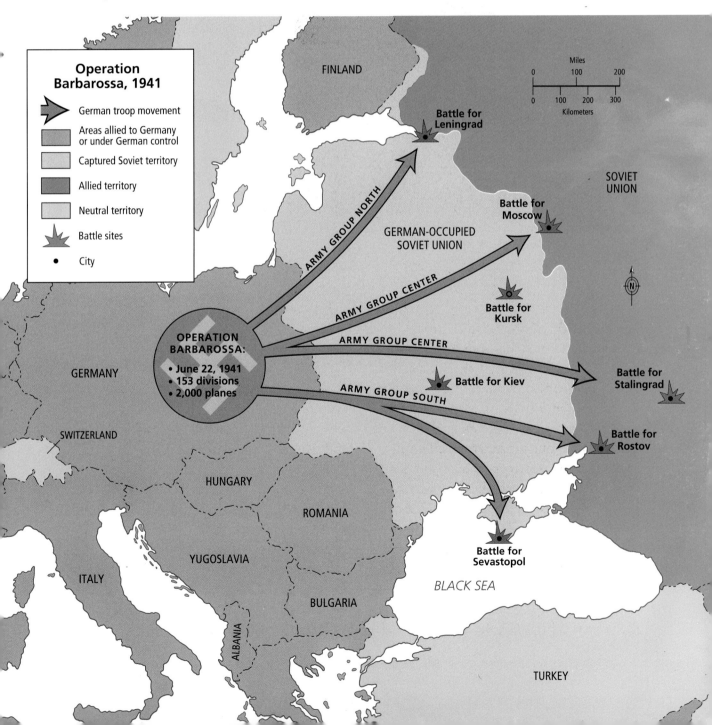

Operation Barbarossa, 1941

- German troop movement
- Areas allied to Germany or under German control
- Captured Soviet territory
- Allied territory
- Neutral territory
- Battle sites
- City

FINLAND

Battle for Leningrad

SOVIET UNION

ARMY GROUP NORTH

Battle for Moscow

GERMAN-OCCUPIED SOVIET UNION

ARMY GROUP CENTER

Battle for Kursk

ARMY GROUP CENTER

Battle for Stalingrad

OPERATION BARBAROSSA:
- June 22, 1941
- 153 divisions
- 2,000 planes

GERMANY

ARMY GROUP SOUTH

Battle for Kiev

SWITZERLAND

Battle for Rostov

HUNGARY

ROMANIA

YUGOSLAVIA

ITALY

ALBANIA

BULGARIA

Battle for Sevastopol

BLACK SEA

TURKEY

Miles
0   100   200

0   100   200   300
Kilometers

The Holocaust

Two furnaces at the Dachau death camp in Germany. Hitler's plan, "the final solution," was to kill all Jewish people.

In May 1941, Adolf Hitler issued secret orders to kill all Jews under German rule. The Nazis formed special units called Einsatzgruppen to carry out these orders. In an early example of Nazi brutality, in September 1941, two days after the Germans captured Kiev (in modern-day Ukraine), Einsatzgruppe 4A posted a notice for all Jews in the city to report to a street corner. Once assembled, the Jews were marched to a ravine called Babi Yar. The Germans ordered the Jews to strip out of their clothing and shot them, one by one. In 36 hours, the Germans murdered 33,771 Jews. Similar scenes occurred throughout German-occupied lands.

Soon the Germans made the killing more efficient. The Einsatzgruppen rounded up people to be exterminated and loaded them onto trains bound for concentration camps. The strongest inmates were forced into slave labor, only to starve or die from exhaustion. Others underwent cruel medical experiments. But most inmates were systematically murdered. They were stripped and shaved (the hair became stuffing for Nazi pillows), then taken to shower chambers in groups as large as 2,000 people. There they were sprayed with deadly cyanide gas. Once everyone was dead, Nazi guards forced other camp inmates to pull out gold teeth from the mouths of the dead and then burn the bodies in giant furnaces. In less than four years, the Nazis murdered more than 12 million people, nearly half of them Jews. The mass killings are known as the Holocaust.

On November 15, the Germans got within 25 miles of Moscow. It looked as if Guderian might encircle the city. But the Germans could go no farther. They had used up all their supplies and reinforcements. Winter dealt the Germans the crowning blow. Snow fell, and temperatures plummeted to –40°F. Hitler had been so sure of quick success that his supply system had no winter clothing. On December 5, the Germans stopped their advance.

Soviet counterattacks began on December 6. Hitler demanded that his officers hold their positions. Instead, Guderian, Rundstedt, and dozens of other German officers withdrew, against Hitler's orders, to positions offering better defense. As punishment for disobeying him, Hitler removed the officers from command and retired them. In late February 1942, Soviet attacks stopped because the Soviets, too, had run out of men and supplies. Meanwhile, the United States began shipping supplies and equipment to the Soviets.

THE GERMAN SUMMER OFFENSIVE

Both sides prepared to fight again. Desperate for manpower, the Germans brought in whole armies from Hungary, Romania, and Italy to help fight the Soviets. The German offensive started on May 8, 1942. Army Group South had been split into Army Groups A and B. Hitler continued to interfere with the generals, switching panzer units back and forth.

In August and September, the Germans advanced deep into the Caucasus, almost reaching the Caspian Sea. In the Caucasus, they ran out of fuel, which had to be carried forward by camels. Furious with the lack of success, Hitler took command of Army Group A, issuing daily orders from his headquarters in Berlin, Germany's capital.

Hitler ordered the Sixth Army, under General Friedrich Paulus, to take the Soviet city of Stalingrad. Paulus reached the outskirts of Stalingrad in early September, and bitter house-to-house fighting raged in the city until the end of October. On November 19, 1942, the Soviets attacked Romanian and Italian

Battle for Stalingrad

In September 1942, advancing German troops under the command of General Friedrich Paulus reached Stalingrad, Russia. Paulus's men surrounded and took much of the city. It looked like Operation Barbarossa would be a rousing success. Yet the Germans could not take all of the city. They met fierce resistance from Soviet troops, who refused to give up. Starving and low on ammunition, Soviet troops fought for months from street to street, defending even rubbish piles. In the end, Soviet reinforcements reached Stalingrad, and the defenders became the attackers. Paulus and his men were forced to surrender. The battle is considered a major turning point in the war, changing the German advance into retreat.

armies on either side of Stalingrad. They broke through, encircling the city. Hitler ordered the Sixth Army to hold Stalingrad.

Positioned in the rubble of a bombed-out Stalingrad building, Soviet soldiers return fire on German infantry. The Battle for Stalingrad (1942–1944) was intense and bloody, fought street by street and house to house.

Hitler's Europe, 1942

Legend:
- Allied territory
- Axis power
- Area occupied by Germany
- Axis ally
- Neutral nation
- - - - Boundary of Soviet Union, 1941
- - · - Country border

Miles
0 100 200 300

0 200 400
Kilometers

But Paulus was stranded almost 200 miles from the nearest other German unit. Hitler ordered him to fight to the death. On February 2, 1943, however, Paulus surrendered. The Soviets captured his 338,000 soldiers and sent them to prison camps in Siberia, in the desolate northern part of the Soviet Union.

THE SOVIET OFFENSIVE

In late 1942, Hitler finally realized that his armies faced disaster in the Caucasus, and he allowed them to withdraw. The withdrawal left the battle lines basically where they had been at the beginning of the 1942 offensive. The Germans began another offensive on July 5, 1943. They attacked toward the city of Kursk but were stopped in only seven days. The greatly improved Soviet armies, fighting in what they called the Great Patriotic War, faced Hitler's soldiers with confidence.

After stopping the Germans, the Soviets started their own offensive. They attacked with hordes of infantry and tanks supported by masses of artillery. The Soviets suffered heavy casualties but recaptured Kiev on November 6, 1943.

The Soviets attacked around Leningrad on January 15, 1944. At the same time, they moved toward Hungary and Romania. Hitler continued to meddle with his troops, order-ing the defense of every piece of ground to the last man and firing generals he thought withdrew too easily. In June 1944, the Soviets reached the Romanian border.

By this time, the flow of supplies from the United States had increased Soviet power. The United States gave the Soviets more than 385,000 trucks, 7,000 tanks, 14,000 aircraft, 13,000 railroad cars, 2,670,000 tons of petroleum, plus substantial amounts of food for the soldiers. Thanks in part to aid from the United States, Stalin kept up his offensives. He advanced into Poland until his forces reached the suburbs of Warsaw.

Soviet troops move out of a cornfield and advance on German positions during the Soviet offensive of 1943. Hitler's blitzkrieg tactics did not work in the Soviet Union, where his war machine was bogged down by vast terrain, poor weather, and a determined Soviet military.

THE WARSAW UPRISING OF 1944

Germany had conquered Poland in 1939, but the Poles still opposed the Nazis. During German occupation, Polish civilians formed the Polish Underground to resist German rule. These resistance fighters rose up in rebellion and seized Warsaw on August 1, 1944.

The underground remained loyal to their old Polish leaders, many of whom had gone into exile in Britain after the German invasion. But Stalin wanted to put a Communist government in control of Poland. As the Poles fought against the Germans, the Soviet armies withdrew and let the Nazis put down the rebellion. The Germans took two months to do it, destroying the city at the same time. The last of the Polish patriots ended up living, fighting, and dying in sewers, because the city above them had been demolished.

Leaving the Poles to their fate, Stalin attacked Romania on August 20, 1944. On August 25, the Romanians promptly changed sides and joined the Soviets to fight the Germans. Bulgaria withdrew from the war on August 26, but Stalin overran the country anyway. He installed a Communist government there and had it declare war on Germany on September 8.

Members of the Polish Home Army (Polish resistance fighters who were part of the Polish Underground). During the two-month Warsaw Uprising of 1944, the Polish Home Army killed 26,000 German troops before being defeated. The army resisted German occupation throughout Poland during World War II, attacking German targets and supply lines, as well as destroying military equipment.

Joseph Stalin

In terms of brutality, Joseph Stalin *(right)* rivaled Adolf Hitler. Stalin used murder and fear to keep his armies fighting. Soldiers and officers who lost a battle or were suspected of disloyalty were executed or sent to prison camps in Siberia. In many cases, Communist Party officials rounded up officers' families and sent them to Siberia too.

By war's end, more than 10 million people (not including enemy soldiers killed in battle) had died at Soviet hands. The victims included 15,000 Polish intellectuals, professors, and army officers murdered in the Katyn Forest near Smolensk, Russia; 3 million-plus German, Italian, and Hungarian prisoners of war; 2 million or so Westward-leaning politicians and intellectuals in Eastern European states overrun by the Soviets; at least 2 million Soviet soldiers; and at least 5 million Soviet citizens suspected of disloyalty. Most of these victims disappeared, or were sent away, never to be seen again. The exact numbers will never be known.

The Bulgarians attacked German forces in Yugoslavia and Greece. They were joined by Yugoslavian fighters opposed to German occupation. To prevent Communists from seizing the Greek government, British prime minister Winston Churchill landed British troops in Greece on October 4, 1944.

As 1944 drew to a close, the Soviets prepared to invade Germany. The attack on the Soviet Union, hindered by Hitler's poor military and economic decisions, had weakened Germany. Thus Stalin found himself in a position to seize vast areas of Europe and to redraw the map of Eastern Europe to his liking.

4 THE GIANT AWAKENS

As war raged in Europe, the United States, an ocean away, faced its own problems. The Great Depression had hit the United States hard. Economic suffering was foremost in everyone's mind. President Franklin D. Roosevelt, who had taken office in 1933, tried to raise civilian morale and salvage the U.S. economy. He promised "a square deal for every man [fair pay for honest work]." He started or continued giant building projects, such as construction of the Hoover Dam, which provided jobs to thousands of people. He also stabilized banks and the stock market, started the Social Security system, and began dozens of other programs to help the people in the United States.

The United States focused on economic recovery, not the war in Europe. Many people in the United States were isolationists, people who wanted to ignore the rest of the world. They did not want a big military, except for a strong navy to protect U.S. shores. Remembering the sacrifices their soldiers had made in World War I, many people did not want to become involved in another foreign war.

Even as Adolf Hitler rose to power in Germany, most people in the United States could see no threat that justified preparation for war. The heroic U.S. aviator Charles A. Lindbergh, the first man to fly nonstop across the Atlantic Ocean (in 1927), visited Hitler's Germany several times. He came back to the United States with stories of German technical know-how and recovery from the Depression. He was convinced that Hitler was using his power to better the lot of the average German and that he posed no threat to world peace. Lindbergh was very well known in the United States, and people listened to him.

Another prominent isolationist was Senator Gerald Nye. As war loomed in Europe, Nye called for the United States to remain neutral and to prohibit arms shipments to foreign countries. Many clergymen, too, supported the isolationist cause.

> ### EYEWITNESS QUOTE: ISOLATIONISM
>
> **"Frankly and definitely there is danger ahead— danger against which we must prepare. But we well know that we cannot escape it [danger], or the fear of danger, by crawling into bed and pulling the covers over our heads."**
>
> —President Franklin Delano Roosevelt, 1940 radio address

Congress refused to provide money to build up, or even modernize, the U.S. Army. Congress also refused to support any program to prepare U.S. industry to make weapons and other military equipment.

But Germany's occupation of Czechoslovakia in 1938 began to change U.S. attitudes. Alarmed by Hitler's aggression, in the summer of 1939 Congress approved funding for military preparedness programs. In September 1939, Germany invaded Poland. Finally, some people in the United States wanted to fight, or at least actively prepare for war.

President Franklin Delano Roosevelt addresses the public on his decision to back the Neutrality Bill of 1939. Roosevelt believed the United States should join Great Britain and France in declaring war on Germany. Much of Congress and the public, however, believed the United States should remain neutral, or stay out of the war.

President Roosevelt saw that Hitler and Mussolini had plans for world domination. He also worried about the Japanese invasion of China. He believed that war would come to the United States sooner or later, and he was determined to prepare the country for war, whether Congress and the people agreed or not. Using executive orders—laws that do not require congressional approval—Roosevelt began to build a personal staff to oversee industrial preparation for war.

GEARING UP FOR WAR

The U.S. Army was poorly equipped at this time. In early 1940, for instance, it had only 28 new tanks. None of these carried a gun larger than 37mm, and none had the most modern design features. After Hitler invaded France in May 1940, the United States began to reevaluate its plans for tank production. The United States appeared to be in deep trouble. Other than a few railroad locomotive factories, the country didn't even have a building big enough for making tanks.

On Saturday, June 11, 1940, a Roosevelt staff member telephoned K. T. Keller, president of the Chrysler automobile company in Detroit, Michigan. In just six days and without a contract, Keller's engineers drove 700 miles to Rock Island, Illinois, and back. They brought 186 pounds of technical drawings back to Detroit and started designing a factory

to make the tank shown in the drawings. After looking at reports from France, the army changed the tank design to include more modern features. On July 17, 1940, Keller finished his building and manufacturing plans, only to learn that the tank he had to make was different from the original design. Keller's engineers didn't complain. They started anew. They knew, for the sake of the country, that the job had to be done.

Construction of the new Detroit Arsenal started in early September 1940. The final 10,000 drawings for the new M-3 medium tank didn't arrive until the following month. Despite all the problems, five months later, Keller and Chrysler finished the first tank, even though construction had yet to be finished on the building itself!

In the summer of 1940, construction began on four ordnance plants—government-built factories that made ammunition and explosives. Construction started on 25 more plants in 1941. The army asked companies with reputations for strong management to take over ordnance production. Quaker Oats, which normally made food, took over a bomb-loading plant in Nebraska. The Sherwin-Williams Paint Company took over a shell-loading plant in Illinois.

As war material started coming off the production lines, Roosevelt wanted to get U.S. weapons and equipment into the fight overseas. On January 6, 1941, he pro-

EYEWITNESS QUOTE:
U.S. WAR PRODUCTION

"Yes, we are calling upon the resources, the efficiency and the ingenuity of the American manufacturers of war material of all kinds—airplanes and tanks and guns and ships, and all the hundreds of products that go into this material."

—President Franklin Delano Roosevelt, 1940 national radio address

Tanks roll off the assembly line at the Detroit Arsenal in Michigan in early 1940. Although the United States was not yet in the war, Roosevelt and other leaders pushed for the buildup of the U.S. military and the sharing of military equipment with Allied nations.

posed a new program that became known as lend-lease (after the Lend-Lease Act of 1941). He knew that Allied nations defending themselves from aggressors would not be able to pay cash for military equipment. Therefore, Roosevelt said, the United States should provide the Allies with equipment in exchange for a promise to either pay for or return the material after the end of the war. By March 27, Congress had approved the proposal and set aside money to pay

U.S. manufacturers for equipment to be sent overseas.

THE VICTORY PROGRAM

Germany's invasion of the Soviet Union in June 1941 only energized U.S. leaders in Washington, D.C. At a briefing on weapons production, President Roosevelt was told how many tanks the United States was building. When he heard the figure, Roosevelt uttered two words, "Double it!"

On September 11, 1941, Roosevelt's staff wrote a plan called the Victory Program, based on Roosevelt's instructions. It called for tremendous increases in military production, with totals that would be enough to equip the armed forces of nearly all Allied nations. But the plan ran into political opposition. Congress objected to the plan's high cost. Pacifists—people who opposed war on religious and moral grounds—objected to the very idea of military production. Businesspeople and workers didn't like the plan either, because they thought it gave the government too much control over the nation's economy.

ATTACK ON PEARL HARBOR

Opposition to Roosevelt's plans changed dramatically in December 1941. At that time, the U.S. Pacific fleet was anchored in Pearl Harbor, Hawaii, in the Pacific Ocean. Japanese leaders believed the United States was a threat to Japan's desire to dominate China and the Far East. They thought that destroying the U.S. fleet would force the United States to seek peace and leave Japan alone. Without consulting Germany or Italy, Japan attacked the U.S. fleet in Pearl Harbor on Sunday, December 7. Eight U.S. battleships were damaged or sunk, hundreds of planes were destroyed, and more than 2,200 soldiers and sailors were killed.

But the United States did not seek peace. People were outraged. President Roosevelt spoke before Congress on

> ### EYEWITNESS QUOTE: A REQUEST FOR WAR
>
> **"I ask that the Congress declare that since the unprovoked and dastardly attack by Japan on Sunday, December 7, a state of war has existed between the United States and the Japanese empire."**
>
> —President Franklin Delano Roosevelt, 1941 congressional address

December 8, and Congress immediately declared war on Japan. Within three days, Congress had also declared war on Germany and Italy. U.S. politicians previously opposed to war quickly switched positions. Even the outspoken isolationist Charles Lindbergh volunteered to fight.

ORGANIZING FOR WAR

President Roosevelt and British prime minister Churchill met to make plans to fight the Axis. Their first meeting, called Arcadia, started in Washington, D.C., on December 24, 1941. At that conference, Roosevelt and Churchill agreed to form a coalition, or a partnership, in which each country would work together to fight the same enemy. The two leaders ordered their highest-ranking military leaders, the U.S. Joint Chiefs of Staff (JCS) and the British Chiefs of Staff (BCS), to form the Combined Chiefs of Staff (CCS). This group would direct the combined Allied armies, navies, and air forces.

The giant, the United States, was fully awake. Though war had just been declared, U.S. industry was in its third year of buildup. Training bases were under construction. After the attack on Pearl Harbor, millions of men volunteered or were drafted for military service. Other men—and women, too—took jobs in weapons factories. People in the United States were unified and moving toward a single goal, the defeat of the Axis.

A Resolution of War

December 11, 1941

To the Congress of the United States:

On the morning of Dec. 11 the Government of Germany, pursuing its course of world conquest, declared war against the United States. The long-known and the long-expected has thus taken place. The forces endeavoring to enslave the entire world now are moving toward this hemisphere. Never before has there been a greater challenge to life, liberty and civilization. Delay invites great danger. Rapid and united effort by all of the peoples of the world who are determined to remain free will insure a world victory of the forces of justice and of righteousness over the forces of savagery and of barbarism. Italy also has declared war against the United States.

The Japanese attack on Pearl Harbor (above) on December 7, 1941, prompted the United States to declare war against the Axis powers (Germany, Italy, and Japan).

I therefore request the Congress to recognize a state of war between the United States and Germany, and between the United States and Italy.

Franklin D. Roosevelt

U.S. Congress War Resolution of 1941

Declaring that a state of war exists between the Government of Germany and the government and the people of the United States and making provision to prosecute the same.

Whereas the Government of Germany has formally declared war against the government and the people of the United States of America:

Therefore, be it resolved by the Senate and House of Representatives of the United States of America in Congress assembled, that the state of war between the United States and the Government of Germany which has thus been thrust upon the United States is hereby formally declared; and the President is hereby authorized and directed to employ the entire naval and military forces of the government to carry on war against the Government of Germany; and to bring the conflict to a successful termination, all of the resources of the country are hereby pledged by the Congress of the United States.

THE BATTLE
5 OF THE ATLANTIC

As an island nation, Great Britain relied on its merchant ships—ships that carried consumer and industrial goods—for survival. It imported raw materials and exported manufactured products by sea. In the event of war, any weapons and supplies Britain purchased, and any invasion it wanted to make, also had to move by sea. Britain had to maintain absolute control of the sea to survive. The Germans were determined to challenge this control.

When Hitler invaded Poland, he already had warships and U-boats, or submarines, at sea. After Britain declared war on Germany on September 3, 1939, the Germans attacked British merchant ships. For protection, the British ships banded together in groups called convoys. Warships escorted the convoys, defending them against German submarines. However, convoys didn't solve the whole problem because the British navy didn't have enough warships for escort duty. It could only provide escorts close to the British Isles. Britain suffered heavy merchant ship losses—754,686 tons of merchant shipping in 1939 (tonnage is the weight of the water displaced by the entire ship, plus cargo).

Although the situation at sea looked bad for Britain, the Germans also had a problem: too few ports with access to the Atlantic Ocean. But Germany's conquest of Norway in April 1940 and France in June 1940 gave Hitler the ports he needed.

The Tonnage Theory

German admiral Karl Doenitz believed in the tonnage theory, which stated that consistently sinking 700,000 tons of Allied merchant shipping per month would force the Allies (especially Britain) to seek peace. This theory dominated the struggle to control the Atlantic shipping lanes, and tons became the measure of success or failure by both sides.

German U-boats then had much better access to the sea.

THE GERMAN HAPPY TIME

From June to December 1940, German U-boats enjoyed what German sailors called the first "happy time." The new ports allowed them to stay at sea longer and attack more convoys. The British had so few escort warships that they could use only one or two to protect a convoy that might contain more than 30 merchant ships.

Admiral Karl Doenitz

During this time, Admiral Karl Doenitz, commander of German U-boats, perfected his wolf pack tactics. He first used this technique against British convoy SC-7. Doenitz positioned five U-boats around the convoy. Surfacing at night, the U-boats attacked from all directions—even from inside the convoy itself.

German U-boats docked at a secret submarine base. In the late 1930s and early 1940s, German U-boat crews controlled the Atlantic, attacking Allied merchant and military vessels at will.

Just moments after being torpedoed by a German U-boat, a merchant ship burns and sinks. In the early 1940s, German U-boats could sneak into ship convoys undetected.

The Germans sank 22 of the 34 merchant ships in SC-7. They had similar success against other convoys. By the end of 1940, Britain and its allies had lost 3,654,511 tons of merchant shipping.

In the dark, a surfaced U-boat was difficult to see. So German wolf packs attacked at night, on the surface. But Doenitz didn't realize how far the Allies had come in developing radar, a new technology that could detect U-boats even in complete darkness. Radar is a system that sends out a radio signal. When that signal hits an object, it bounces back, telling the radar operator where the object is. Once escort warships began to carry radar, in 1941, they could detect surfaced U-boats at night.

In July 1941, the United States took over the defense of Iceland, a small island in the North Atlantic. The U.S. Navy built bases, and U.S. warships began convoy escort duties from Icelandic ports. The battle shifted against Doenitz.

The Germans lost 35 U-boats in 1941. Because Hitler hadn't increased his weapons production, he couldn't build enough new boats to replace his losses. The new crews were inexperienced and less effective than earlier crews. Merchant ship losses shrank from an average of 241,000 tons per month at the beginning of 1941 to 120,000 tons per month at the end of the year.

On October 31, 1941, a U-boat sank the U.S. destroyer *Reuben James,* and the United States found itself unofficially at war in the Atlantic. After the United States declared war on Germany in December 1941, Doenitz sent his U-boats to the Atlantic coast of the United States. The U.S. Navy escorted convoys across the Atlantic but not between individual U.S. ports. Thus merchant ships sailing from one Atlantic coast city to another were undefended, and German U-boat sailors enjoyed a second "happy time." The Germans sank hundreds of U.S. ships in the first half of 1942. U.S. losses averaged 519,000 tons per month. Further, Germany was finally producing more U-boats—so many that the total number kept increasing, in spite of losses.

TECHNOLOGY REVERSES THE BATTLE

U.S. production of both warships and merchant ships increased at a dramatic rate in late 1942. Shipyards in the United States also launched two new types of warships that year. The escort aircraft carrier, built on a merchant ship hull, carried only 12 to 18 planes. That wasn't a lot compared to typical warships, which carried more than 70 planes, but it was enough to fly around a convoy and attack any U-boat sailing on the surface. The other new warship, the destroyer escort, was less heavily armed and slower than a regular destroyer, but it could still sink a U-boat. Both new ships were much easier and cheaper to build than regular destroyers.

The U.S.-made B-24 Liberator (a four-engine bomber) also rolled off production lines in increasing numbers. The navy experimented by removing the plane's heavy steel armor (protective plating) and machine guns, reducing its bomb load, and using the savings in weight to carry extra fuel. The result was an aircraft that had a range of 2,600 nautical miles. It was called the VLR, for "very long range."

The escort carrier **U.S.S.** *Bogue* steams through the Atlantic Ocean, with its aircraft out on patrol. Planes could take off from and land on the flat landing strips of the escort carriers, or "baby flat tops," to protect shipping convoys or to attack targets on land.

WOMEN AND THE WAR EFFORT

Before World War II, many people in the United States believed that women belonged at home, working as wives and mothers. But as men enlisted to fight, someone had to run the nation's factories. So manpower turned into womanpower. Unused to working outside the home, however, many women needed convincing. Slogans such as "If you can drive a car, you can run a machine" encouraged women to try factory work.

Female riveters, electricians, and machine operators built the tanks, warships, and airplanes the troops needed. Women welded steel, operated cranes, and even flew airplanes. Harriet Williamson was working as a welder in an Illinois shipyard when her husband was killed in a munitions plant explosion. Widowed with three children, Williamson stuck with her work. When the first tank-landing ship was completed at her shipyard, she got the honor of smashing the champagne bottle to launch the ship.

Many female factory workers had young children who needed day care when their mothers worked. So a group called the American Women's Voluntary Services staffed day care centers at factories and commuter railroad stations. Every morning, female workers could drop their children at these centers, where other women cared for them at no pay.

A popular song praised "Rosie the Riveter"—a nickname for the female factory worker—and her contributions to the war effort. More than 18 million U.S. women made that effort. They took pride in their work and in their paychecks. Although they earned less than men for the same jobs, those paychecks gave women an economic freedom they had never known before.

The military didn't have enough men to wage such a big war. So the army formed the Women's Army Corps (WAC) and named Oveta Culp Hobby

Artist Norman Rockwell's portrayal of Rosie the Riveter (rivet gun on her lap) taking a lunch break. Rosie, a symbol of the typical female factory worker, appeared on magazines and posters with many different looks.

WACs (members of the Women's Army Corps) boarding a ship bound for Europe. The work of WACs and other servicewomen helped keep the Allied war machine operating smoothly, saving countless servicemen in combat.

as its director. But the U.S. government feared that women dying in combat would horrify the public, so WACs weren't allowed to hold combat jobs. Instead, WAC radio and teletype operators relayed messages at air bases and army headquarters. WACs also served as mechanics, laboratory technicians, and drivers. U.S. general Dwight D. Eisenhower had a WAC driver in 1944. In the Fifth Army alone, 27 WACs received medals for honorable service.

Even though they couldn't join combat units, some women died for their country. The WAFS (Women's Auxiliary Ferrying Squadron) delivered bombers and fighters to airfields in Great Britain and the Soviet Union. By flying noncombat missions, WAFS freed male pilots to fly in combat. Women pilots often flew without navigators, radios, or complete technical gear (which was to be added at the airfields). Those flying to the Soviet Union had to cross Canada and Alaska. Without navigators, the female pilots flew low under the clouds, using only visual landmarks as guides. In emergencies, the pilots had no radios with which to call for help. Thirty-eight WAFS were killed when their planes crashed on ferrying missions.

Thousands of registered nurses joined the Navy and Army Nurse Corps during the war, leaving a shortage of nurses in the United States. Nurses in training stepped in to fill that gap. Called the Cadet Nurse Corps, this group numbered more than 112,000.

Many other women on the home front held civil defense positions—running air-raid shelters, fighting fires, and patrolling the skies for enemy planes. Others worked for organizations such as the United Service Organizations (USO), which provided entertainment and social and recreational services to soldiers. The women of World War II were often called "home front warriors," and indeed they were.

Crewmen aboard a **U.S. destroyer escort** make a killing hit with depth charges on a German U-boat. The explosives *(left)* were fired into the ocean and then sank to a preset depth, where seamen believed a sub was lurking. The convoy under protection of this destroyer is visible in the background.

THE ATLANTIC CONVOY CONFERENCE

In March 1943, Admiral Doenitz concentrated 40 U-boats against two Allied convoys. The Germans sank 21 ships. Total Allied shipping losses for the month topped 627,000 tons. A crisis was clearly at hand.

Admiral Ernest J. King, chief of all U.S. naval forces, called for the Atlantic Convoy Conference in Washington. At this conference, he made major changes in the way the Allies fought in the Atlantic. He split the ocean into areas of responsibility for the Canadian, British, and U.S. navies. Regardless of whose merchant ships sailed through an area, the nation responsible for that area had to patrol it and provide convoy escorts. King distributed VLRs among the Allies so that they could fly continuous patrols over almost the entire Atlantic. He assigned new destroyer escorts and escort carriers to protect convoys.

German U-boats sent encoded radio messages to Doenitz on a daily basis. But the Germans didn't know that the Allies had broken their code. Based on the decoded messages, the Allies made a file on each U-boat, including the number of torpedoes it had on board. The Allies also developed a device called a high-frequency direction finder, nicknamed Huff-Duff. This device could intercept a radio signal and tell the precise direction from which it had come. King installed these units on nearly every piece of shoreline under Allied control.

King established the Tenth Fleet and ordered it to coordinate all antisubmarine activities. This work included taking reports from Huff-Duff stations and plotting them on a map. In this way, the Allies knew what each U-boat was doing and its exact location at the time it sent a message. For the first time, Allied ships could go on hunting trips, looking for U-boats, rather than waiting for U-boats to attack a convoy.

DESTROYING THE WOLF PACKS

In late April 1943, Doenitz sent 60 U-boats to attack an Allied convoy. This time, King's ideas paid off. The convoy lost 12 merchant ships, but it sank seven U-boats. Doenitz mounted furious attacks on convoys throughout May, but merchant ship losses actually decreased, and Doenitz lost 41 U-boats in May alone. In the last four months of 1943, the Germans lost 62 U-boats.

In 1944 Germany struck back with a new technology: the snorkel. This pipelike device allowed a submerged U-boat to run its diesel engines underwater, instead of relying on less powerful batteries and electric motors. But Allied air patrols and U.S. carrier groups, all equipped with radar, covered the Atlantic so closely that they could even detect snorkels. In the last seven months of 1944, Doenitz lost 140 U-boats.

In 1945 ever-increasing numbers of Allied warships roamed the seas. VLR aircraft patrolled the Atlantic around the clock. With the Tenth Fleet's Huff-Duff, a U-boat sending a message would have its position plotted and broadcast to all patrol aircraft and warships within minutes. Between January 1 and May 7, 1945, 151 U-boats went to the bottom.

The conflict at sea came to be called the Battle of the Atlantic. It lasted the entire war. Although success seesawed back and forth, in the end the Allies controlled the sea.

A German U-boat struggles to stay afloat after taking heavy damage during an Allied sub hunt. By 1944 destroyers, VLR aircraft, radar, and sonar made it nearly impossible for U-boat crews to hide their boats.

THE UNITED STATES
6 GETS IN THE FIGHT

At the Arcadia conference in Washington, D.C., Franklin Roosevelt and Winston Churchill decided that the Allies would invade North Africa. The United States had actually preferred a different approach. It wanted to invade France and then Germany at the earliest opportunity, then turn to fight the Japanese in the Pacific. But in the end, Roosevelt decided to go along with Churchill's plan to invade North Africa first. An invasion of France would come later.

In North Africa, Erwin Rommel's Afrika Korps had been giving the British fits. Rommel charged into Egypt and reached El Alamein, only 50 miles from the Nile River. But then Rommel ran completely out of supplies, and both sides fell into a stalemate in July 1942. In August 1942, General Harold Alexander took command of all British forces in North Africa. He put Bernard Montgomery in command of the British Eighth Army at El Alamein. On August 31, despite a lack of supplies, Rommel attacked again. Montgomery didn't fully understand the new mobile war, and he dug his tanks into the sand like a series of independent forts. But Rommel had so little gasoline that he literally couldn't drive around them to strike the British rear. He had to halt his attack.

U.S. supplies flowed to Montgomery, including the first new M-4 Sherman tanks from the Detroit Arsenal in Michigan.

Montgomery started the Battle of El Alamein on October 23, 1942. Using colonial infantry (troops from Australia, New Zealand, South Africa, and India) and great concentrations of artillery, he launched attack after attack into German mines and barbed wire. In 12 days, Montgomery advanced only two miles over a narrow front. But Rommel couldn't hold out forever without supplies, and he finally fell back. Eventually, Montgomery advanced across Libya. Rommel retreated into Tunisia, where he finally received replacements and supplies.

THE INVASION OF NORTH AFRICA

A few months earlier, on June 24, 1942, the Joint Chiefs of Staff made General Dwight D. Eisenhower commander of all U.S. forces in Europe and sent him to London. One of his jobs was the overall command of the invasion of North Africa. The plan called for landings at three places: Casablanca in Morocco and Oran and Algiers in Algeria. The enemy at all three landing points would be French, under orders of the German-controlled French government at Vichy. Arguments within the Combined Chiefs of Staff prevented any coordinated efforts, however. The British Chiefs of Staff sent most of its available forces to Alexander and Montgomery instead of to Eisenhower. Some British forces would help at Algiers, but the rest of the invasion force would be U.S. troops.

General George Marshall, chief of staff of the U.S. Army, put General George S. Patton in command of the invasion at Casablanca, Morocco.

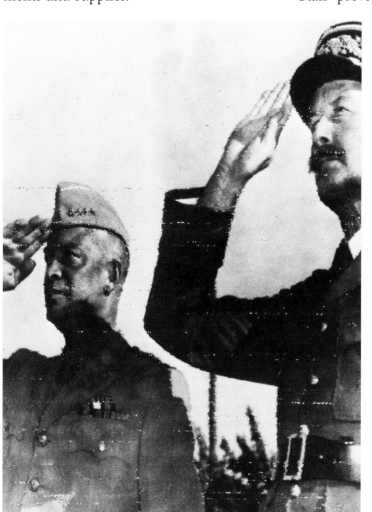

General Dwight D. Eisenhower (left), commander in chief of Allied armies in Africa, and General Henri-Honoré Giraud (right), commander of the Free French forces in Africa, salute their nations' flags at Allied headquarters in Algiers, Algeria. The Allied invasion of North Africa was made up of U.S., British, and Free French troops.

SOLDIERS, UNIFORMS, AND WEAPONS

On September 16, 1940, the U.S. Congress passed the Selective Training and Service Act. This law created the draft, a system for registering and calling up young men for military service. All men in the United States between 21 and 35 were required to register for the draft, the first peacetime draft in U.S. history. Approximately 60 percent of the soldiers who served in World War II were drafted into the military. The others volunteered. U.S. soldiers came from all walks of life.

The U.S. soldier was clothed from head to foot (including socks and underwear) with government-issued items, leading to his nickname of "GI." The standard winter field uniform consisted of a short woolen jacket with two pockets on the front, heavy waist-high brown trousers, and boots. Officers wore pins on their shoulders and collars, indicating their rank. The enlisted man's rank was indicated by sleeve patches. In combat, everyone wore an olive green field jacket, canvas gaiters (leg coverings) below the knees, and a brown helmet with a camouflage netting on top. A webbed belt around the waist held the soldier's canteen, bayonet, and a bandage for dressing wounds.

Each GI underwent basic training in the United States, plus advanced training that focused on his specific job. Altogether, training lasted 16 to 20 weeks. Then the GI

U.S. infantrymen in their winter field gear receive daily rations.

was assigned to a combat unit, where he underwent refresher training.

The GI's rifle, the M-1, was the best in the war. For every GI fighting with an M-1, three to eight other soldiers fired in support. They used automatic rifles, bazookas, machine guns, mortars, tanks, antitank guns, and field artillery. In combat the mortars and field artillery fired from behind the GIs, over their heads, raining explosive shells on the enemy.

German soldiers also came from all walks of life, and many were draftees. The typical German infantryman wore knee-high, square-toed black boots. The tops of the boots fit loosely, allowing soldiers to tuck in their pants. The German field uniform was dark gray green, with a thigh-length coat, cinched at the waist with a black leather belt. The German helmet was a dark steel gray. Its front rim flared out slightly and angled downward at the ears.

German infantrymen receive medical care following a scouting patrol.

The German soldier's weapons and equipment were well designed and well made. He had excellent support from machine guns but did not have as much artillery support as the GI had. Also, the German supply system was always struggling. Most infantry divisions moved supplies in horse-drawn wagons instead of trucks. As U.S. bombing destroyed more factories, German equipment declined in quality. The poor supply situation, particularly on the Russian front, meant that the German infantryman never got as much ammunition, weaponry, and winter clothing as he needed.

Regardless of equipment, it took brave men, on both sides, to fight and win. German soldiers wanted to fight for a number of reasons, such as to protect civilians from British bombing and from Soviet invasion. German troops emphasized teamwork and loyalty to friends. The desire to never let down one's mates ran strong among German infantrymen. This attitude allowed them to accomplish feats out of proportion to their sometimes meager equipment and support. The GI was inspired by these same feelings of loyalty and fellowship, plus the belief that he was fighting for justice and freedom.

Stationed in Norfolk, Virginia, Patton had just 100 days to assemble, organize, and equip an invasion army. This army was then to sail across 2,500 miles of ocean and invade a hostile shore, about which the invaders knew little. No invasion so large or so far away had ever been attempted in the history of warfare. Patton's staff planned the landing using little more than travel guides and tourist maps. On October 25, 1942, Patton set sail with 40,000 men aboard 36 transport ships with an escort of 68 warships.

On November 5, 1942, Eisenhower moved his headquarters to Gibraltar, a

> **EYEWITNESS QUOTE:
> ON THE ALLIED INVASION
> OF NORTH AFRICA**
>
> "I will leave the beaches
> either a conqueror
> or a corpse."
>
> —**General George Patton,
> before the invasion
> of North Africa, 1942**

British colony in the southern part of Spain. From there, he would command the entire invasion. The invasion of Algeria and Morocco began on November 8. Patton's forces at Casablanca immediately met heavy resistance from French troops. After hard fighting, Patton seized Casablanca, and the French surrendered on November 11. The landings at Oran and Algiers met much less resistance and succeeded easily. After a few days of fighting, the French switched sides and joined the Allies.

Eisenhower ordered Patton to hold Morocco and ordered his other forces to move inland, across Algeria and into Tunisia. But Eisenhower commanded a mixture of U.S., British, and French troops, who weren't used to working together. It took them until January 1, 1943, to reach the Tunisian border.

On February 4, 1943, the Combined Chiefs of Staff gave Eisenhower command of all Allied forces (land, sea, and air) in North Africa. He placed Harold Alexander in command of the land forces, including Montgomery's army in Libya and other Allied armies poised on the border of Tunisia, located between Algeria and Libya. Eisenhower ordered Alexander to attack, but Rommel struck first. He hit the United States' II Corps on February 14, getting through the Kasserine Pass in central Tunisia. Rommel defeated the U.S. troops, but lack of support from other German and Italian units forced him to withdraw.

General Patton surveys a battlefield in North Africa. Tank commanders Patton and Rommel matched wits for control of the region.

MINORITIES AT HOME AND OVERSEAS

During World War II, racial prejudice was strong in the United States. Many whites didn't trust African American soldiers to serve under fire. The military kept units segregated, meaning that black and white soldiers were not allowed to train, live, or fight together. The military restricted most black soldiers to menial jobs such as unloading ships, driving trucks, or cooking, or to high-risk jobs such as searching for mines. From the beginning, however, there were exceptions.

In July 1941, the Army Air Corps began training African American aviation cadets at Tuskegee, Alabama. The first graduating cadets became the all-black 99th Fighter Squadron, which later expanded into the 332nd Fighter Group. Called the Tuskegee Airmen, these aviators served with distinction in North Africa and Europe.

By late 1944, casualties in U.S. infantry units were so high that General Eisenhower called for black volunteers to join combat units. Thus white platoons fought side by side with black platoons. Relying on each other in combat made many soldiers color blind by the time victory was declared.

Since Germany, Italy, and Japan were enemies of the United States, people in the United States of German, Italian, and Japanese descent were treated with suspicion and discrimination during the war. The Japanese were treated most harshly. After Japan attacked the United States in 1941, the U.S. government forced more than 100,000 Nisei (Japanese Americans) to relocate to prison camps in the western United States for the rest of the war. Many Italians were also jailed in California camps, but they were released after a short time.

Despite the fact that their families were mistreated and even imprisoned, thousands of German, Italian, and Japanese Americans, including more than 8,000 Nisei, enlisted in the U.S. military during the war. The all-Japanese American 442nd Infantry Regiment fought bravely in France and Italy, becoming one of the most decorated U.S. regiments of the war.

African American Seabees train for combat. Though the men were combat trained, they were never officially allowed to fight. Instead, the U.S. Navy assigned Seabee battalions to hazardous duty working with high explosives and scouting minefields.

German prisoners of war march to an Allied containment camp in North Africa. The success of the Allies in the region was a glimmer of hope in a war that had mostly gone according to plan for Hitler.

Eisenhower called Patton in from Morocco and placed him in command of the battered II Corps. Patton immediately restored fighting morale and discipline. The invasion of Sicily, an island off the Italian coast, was the next critical objective. On April 15, Eisenhower ordered Patton to plan the Sicilian invasion. He put Omar N. Bradley in command of II Corps.

The Allies then attacked into Tunisia. The Germans and Italians fought well until early May. The Italian navy had been supplying the Axis forces. But Allied air attacks from new bases in North Africa made it impossible for the Italian navy to continue operations. The last Axis forces in Tunisia surrendered on May 13, 1943.

THE INVASION OF SICILY

On July 10, 1943, Patton's Seventh Army and Montgomery's Eighth Army landed in Sicily side by side, both under the command of Alexander's 15th Army Group. At first, Patton protected Montgomery's left flank as the British advanced up the coast of Sicily to the city of Messina. Messina was the closest point to the Italian mainland, and its capture would cut off any Axis forces left in Sicily.

Montgomery's advance averaged barely two miles per day. Alexander changed his plans and ordered Patton to break to the west. Patton asked for permission to take the city of Palermo and then attack along the north coast of Sicily toward Messina.

Alexander approved, and Patton made the move brilliantly. In four days, his 3rd Infantry Division fought the 100 miles to Palermo—on foot. He captured the city on July 22.

Rather than fight and die for the Axis, Mussolini's political party and rebellious Italian generals overthrew and arrested Mussolini on July 25, 1943. Marshal Pietro Badoglio took over the Italian government. On August 3, Badoglio ordered Italian forces to retreat from Sicily. The Germans followed and evacuated Messina on August 17.

Hitler feared an Italian collapse. In August he sent German troops into Italy to disarm the Italian army to prevent it from joining the Allies. In fact, Italy secretly signed a cease-fire agreement with the Allies on September 3, 1943. The JCS wanted to save its resources for an invasion of France.

However, with Hitler trying to occupy Italy, the JCS agreed with the BCS to invade Italy. The U.S. Fifth Army, commanded by General Mark Clark, invaded at Salerno on September 9.

At a meeting called the Quadrant Conference, held in Quebec, Canada, in August 1943, the CCS approved the invasion of France. They gave the invasion the code name Operation Overlord and ordered Eisenhower to England to plan it. Before he left the Mediterranean, Eisenhower had one job remaining. General Patton had lost his temper twice while visiting military field hospitals. He had struck three soldiers, accusing them of cowardice. He had even threatened to have them shot. Eisenhower hated to lose Patton, but he couldn't excuse the general's behavior. Eisenhower relieved Patton of command.

Greeted by Italian citizens, U.S. troops roll into the city of Palermo, Italy, on the backs of their Sherman tanks on July 23, 1943. Italian forces had surrendered the city to Patton and his soldiers the day before.

Daniel Inouye and the "Go for Broke" Regiment

Daniel Inouye (IN-oh-way) was 17 years old when the Japanese attacked Hawaii, his home, in 1941. About a year later, Inouye enlisted in the U.S. Army. He was assigned to the all–Japanese American 442nd Infantry Regiment, nicknamed the "Go for Broke" regiment. The 442nd fought in eight major campaigns in Italy, France, and Germany. It became one of the most highly decorated units in military history. Ironically, the soldiers of the 442nd fought bravely for the

Members of the Japanese American "Go for Broke Regiment," in which Inouye served, receive honors in 1944.

United States at the same time many of their relatives, viewed as dangerous because of their Japanese heritage, were imprisoned in camps in the western United States.

Among the unit's many fine soldiers, Daniel Inouye stood out. He quickly received a series of promotions. Fighting in Italy, Inouye was shot through the abdomen, but he continued to lead his platoon against a German machine-gun nest. He kept shooting and throwing grenades, even as a German grenade shattered his right arm and a bullet pierced his leg.

When he was discharged from the army, Inouye was a captain. He returned home with a Distinguished Service Cross, a Bronze Star, a Purple Heart, and 12 other medals and citations. Inouye became Hawaii's first congressman in 1959 and a U.S. senator in 1962. In 2000, he and 21 other Asian American World War II heroes had their citations upgraded to Medals of Honor, the highest U.S. military award for valor.

THE CAIRO-TEHRAN CONFERENCES

Operations in Italy went poorly. The terrain favored the German defenders and resulted in heavy Allied casualties. In late 1943, San Pietro, Monte Cassino, and other Italian towns and cities became household words in the United States because so many U.S. soldiers died there. The BCS felt the United States' sacrifice was worthwhile, because the fighting in Italy prevented German forces from being used elsewhere. But many on the JCS believed that fighting in Italy was wasteful.

This disagreement came to a head at conferences in Cairo, Egypt, and Tehran, Iran.

Roosevelt, Churchill, and the CCS met in Cairo in November 1943. They scheduled a meeting with Stalin in Tehran immediately thereafter. The United States and Great Britain had a showdown at Cairo. The British insisted on more operations in the Mediterranean region and the Balkans. Churchill said that Italy and the Balkans were soft—vulnerable and weakly defended. He argued that the Allies should attack Germany from the south.

These demands enraged the JCS. The terrain in the Balkans was anything but soft. Germany was also protected on its southern border by the neutral nation of Switzerland and by Austria, with the highest mountains in Europe. The JCS believed that the only pathway to the heart of Germany was across France. The United States was also fighting a war with Japan in the Pacific Ocean. The demand for ships, men, and planes in the Pacific appeared overwhelming. The United States needed to win the war in Europe quickly and then turn its attention to Japan.

In Tehran, Stalin insisted on a main invasion of northern France from Britain and a secondary invasion of southern France from the Mediterranean. He believed this was the fastest way to defeat Germany. Stalin promised to declare war on Japan once Germany was defeated. The Cairo-Tehran meetings ended with the decision to fight in Italy, yet not to delay the invasion of France. The meetings also bred intense misunderstanding and distrust among the Allies. The coalition would stay together, but it was strained.

LANDING AT ANZIO BEACH

Bitter fighting in Italy continued. Casualties mounted, and troops made little progress. U.S. forces landed behind German lines at Anzio, Italy, near Rome, on January 22, 1944. But the Germans' tough defense kept the U.S. troops bottled up near the beach.

Mustering all possible strength (including U.S., British, Polish, Indian, French, South African, Moroccan, and Algerian divisions), Alexander managed to break through German lines to Anzio. The U.S. troops captured Rome on June 4, 1944. But mountains lay ahead of them in northern Italy. U.S. commanders knew it would cost high casualties just to reach Switzerland, and U.S. troops still wouldn't be near Germany. Italy wasn't the pathway to the heart of Germany after all.

Allied landing craft and a supply ship race toward Anzio Beach during the invasion of Italy during the summer of 1944.

THE AIR WAR

7

The air war against Germany began in July 1941 with the first British bombing of Germany. The British bombed in daylight and suffered heavy losses because German fighter pilots and antiaircraft troops could see them. So the British switched to bombing at night.

Sir Arthur Harris, chief of the British Bomber Command, promoted a technique called area bombing. Rather than trying to hit specific targets, such as factories, British bombers would attack an entire city at night. In this way, they could reduce the city to rubble. If they destroyed factories in the process, fine. If not, they could still kill the civilians who worked in the factories or, failing that, kill workers'

families, destroy their homes, and make them miserable.

Harris wanted to send 1,000 bombers to one city all at once. He launched the first such raid on Cologne, Germany, on May 30, 1942. The raid killed 486 people and destroyed more than 18,000 buildings. Incendiary bombs, or bombs designed to start fires, caused the worst devastation. Harris carried out 17 such raids in 1942.

PRECISION BOMBING

In contrast to the British, U.S. commanders believed in daylight bombing to accurately hit specific targets. U.S. pilots could do this successfully with the B-17 bomber, designed for this precision daylight role.

The B-17 was built tough. It had 10 (later 13) .50-caliber machine guns. Flying in tight formation, these bombers could fire a hail of bullets at any enemy fighter bold enough to attack. Further, the United States had the Norden bombsight, an aiming device that helped bombardiers line up on targets and know when to release bombs. The Norden took the plane's speed, altitude, and other factors into account. No other nation had such an accurate bombsight.

In February 1942, General Ira C. Eaker arrived in England to build airfields for the U.S. Eighth Air Force. While the British continued to push for area bombing, Eaker chose to precisely target enemy airfields, U-boat docks, railroad yards, and other industrial and military facilities.

Courage and Devotion

In one airstrike on Germany, U.S. lieutenant Jack W. Mathis was the lead bombardier (airman responsible for aiming and releasing bombs) in a combat box (bomber formation). Just as he started his straight and level bomb run, an explosive antiaircraft shell hit his plane. The shell splinters tore through Mathis's body. He couldn't stop to care for himself because the accuracy of the bombing run depended on him. He put the bombs on target, and the rest of the box followed suit. After the B-17 turned for home, the navigator went to check on Mathis in the nose of the B-17. He lay slumped forward. He had bled to death, his eye still pressed to his bombsight.

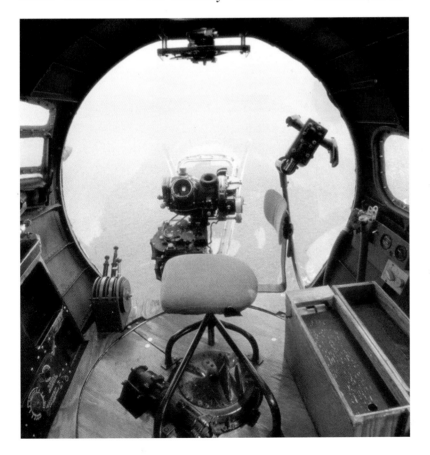

The bombardier's station in the nose of a B-17 bomber. The Norden bombsight (front center) made the B-17 a very accurate bomber.

HARDWARE AND ARMAMENTS

Technological innovation is extremely important in winning a war. The side with the best (and most) weapons and equipment has a tremendous advantage. U.S. industry gave the U.S. soldier and sailor that advantage.

An 8-inch U.S. howitzer (cannon)

Artillery For indirect artillery (fired when the gunner cannot see his target and must fire over obstacles such as hills to hit the enemy), the U.S. 105mm and 8-inch cannons had no equal. Their design, along with their ammunition, gave accuracy, range, and reliability that no other nation's weapons could match.

Detection equipment The British pioneered radar, but the United States quickly caught up in radar design, quality, and quantity. Radar and underwater listening devices, such as sonar, enabled U.S. ships and planes to detect enemy U-boats and planes in daytime, nighttime, or stormy weather. With this equipment, U.S. forces were able to fire upon U-boats at night, before the Germans even knew anyone was near.

Fuses A fuse is the device in the nose of an artillery shell that makes it explode. The U.S. variable time (VT) fuse had a small radio set that sent out a signal. When a signal bounced back from a preset distance, the shell exploded. Shells exploded while still in the air (instead of after striking something, such as the ground). The shell splinters exploded in all directions, greatly increasing the damage inflicted on enemy infantry. No other army had this advantage.

Planes The German Messerschmitt 109 and Focke-Wulf 190, along with the British Spitfire, were good fighters. However, the U.S. P-47 and P-51 were superior to them all. Heavier, faster, and tougher than other nation's planes, armored, and carrying .50-caliber machine guns, U.S. fighters set a standard that others could not match. As for bombers, the U.S. B-17 and B-24 were vastly superior in bombing accuracy, armor, and machine guns.

U.S. P-51 Mustang

Ships U.S. naval engineers ruled the seas. The easily made yet efficient destroyer escorts and escort carriers cleared the Atlantic of U-boats. The landing ship tank (LST), a U.S. oceangoing vessel, sailed onto beaches and opened at the bow (front), allowing tanks in its hold to drive out into battle. The LST and other landing craft enabled the Allies to make seaborne invasions whenever needed.

German Messerschmitt 109

The U.S. Liberty ship carried the United States to victory. Designed to carry cargo or fuel, this merchant ship was known for its reliability, sturdiness, and ease of construction. The fastest built Liberty ship was the U.S.S. *Robert E. Perry*. It set sail, laden with cargo, on November 13, 1942, the afternoon of the seventh day after its construction began.

Tanks Germany had some great tanks in the Panther and Tiger (both boasted powerful guns and heavy armor), but they were not the most mechanically reliable and were never made in large numbers. The U.S. M-4 Sherman, despite its thinner armor and smaller gun, stood out. It could fire faster and more accurately than any tank on either side.

U.S. Liberty ships heavily laden with cargo

The crew of a B-17 bomber hits its mark during a U.S. bombing sortie (mission) in the early 1940s. U.S. bomber crews used precision bombing instead of area bombing, preferred by the British.

The United States launched its first bombing raid on August 17, 1942, targeting German-held railroad yards in Rouen, France. Though only 12 B-17 bombers flew the mission, they all hit their targets and returned safely.

But Eaker suffered severe criticism from the British. Despite his bombers' accuracy and success, up to 40 percent of them returned from raids with some damage from German fire. Bombers were often on the ground for repairs. Further, the Germans shot down between 2 and 4 percent of the U.S. bombers on each mission.

But Roosevelt and the JCS supported Eaker and backed his tactics at a conference at Casablanca in January 1943. The BCS made undermining German civilian

The Memphis Belle

The *Memphis Belle*, a B-17 bomber piloted by Captain Robert Morgan, was the first U.S. bomber to successfully fight 25 missions. It completed its last mission on May 17, 1943. In the course of those missions, its crew shot down eight German fighter planes. The *Memphis Belle* left England in June 1943 for a public relations tour of the United States. Two movies have been made about the plane—a 1944 documentary by William Wyler and a 1990 fictionalized drama. Visitors can see the plane on display in Memphis, Tennessee. You can also visit <www.memphisbelle.com> for more information about the plane.

The Terror of War

From late July to early August 1943, Great Britain's Bomber Command hit Hamburg, Germany, with incendiary bombs, creating a huge firestorm. Temperatures rose above 2,000°F. Asphalt streets burned, granite building blocks melted, and people in underground shelters were baked to ashes. More than 50,000 civilians died. The United States participated in a similar firebombing of Dresden, Germany, later in the war.

Workers clear a rubble-filled street in Hamburg, Germany, following the August 1943 firebombing.

morale a secondary objective, thereby allowing Harris to continue his area bombing of German cities.

TRAINING AND TECHNOLOGY

Eaker used the ideas of Air Force colonel Curtis E. LeMay to improve U.S. bombing efficiency. LeMay increased training for navigators, bombardiers, and machine gunners. He put the best navigators and bombardiers in the lead bomber of each combat box (a formation of 18 to 21 aircraft). The whole box followed the leader and dropped their bombs where the lead bombardier dropped his. This system, coupled with technology such as the autopilot (an automatic steering device) and the Norden bombsight, greatly increased Allied bombing accuracy and reduced civilian casualties.

The results were stupendous. On March 18, 1943, 73 bombers struck the submarine yards at Vegesack, Germany. From an altitude of over 20,000 feet, the bombers put 888 of 1,168 bombs within 1,000 feet of the exact center of the target area.

The B-17 itself greatly contributed to the United States' success. The plane could take heavy hits, suffer great damage, and still fly home for repairs. No German fighter planes could take such punishment, especially when the United States shot at them with big .50-caliber machine guns that fired highly destructive armor-piercing and incendiary bullets. German fighters had little armor (protective steel plating), and wounded pilots could not easily bail out of them. Slowly but surely, the United States began to chew up the Luftwaffe.

U.S. bombers also suffered heavy losses, but for every bomber shot down, more bombers arrived from the United States.

THE AMERICAN HOME FRONT

During World War II, the U.S. government and other U.S. institutions created propaganda that inspired citizens to make whatever sacrifices it took to defeat the Axis. Posters and slogans urged people to support their fighting troops in different ways. Hollywood movies such as *They Were Expendable* showed U.S. soldiers dying bravely. Director William Wyler created a documentary film praising the heroism of the crew of the *Memphis Belle,* a bomber. The film featured real footage shot aboard the plane.

Fighting a war is expensive. To raise money, the U.S. government sold war bonds. Purchasing a bond was like lending money to the government. Adults paid between $25 and $10,000 for war bonds, and schoolchildren spent nickels and dimes to buy war stamps.

To save resources for the war effort, the government rationed (restricted purchases of) food and luxuries. Families were issued ration books containing coupons. They could use the coupons for specific purchases of meat, butter, sugar, and other foods—but no more than the allotted amount. The government also rationed gasoline to conserve supplies for military and industrial vehicles.

Encouraged by government posters such as the one above, U.S. citizens planted "Victory Gardens" in backyards and vacant lots, growing their own vegetables and freeing up other food supplies for the troops. Women's magazines printed "Victory Menus" and other tips on how families could make do with less food. Children and adults collected tin foil, cans, cooking pans, and even automobile parts. This scrap metal was then melted down and made into tanks or grenades.

Both men and women—twelve million in the United States—became civil defense volunteers, helping their communities prepare for and prevent enemy attacks. These volunteers, wearing old World War I helmets painted white, included air-raid wardens, plane spotters, firefighters, and first-aid workers. A group called the Civil Air Patrol flew unarmed private planes over the Atlantic, looking for German U-boats.

Many civilians made the ultimate sacrifice during the war—the death of family members in military service. Each U.S. family with men in the military displayed a banner in the window, with one blue star for each serviceman. When soldiers were killed, families replaced the blue stars with gold stars.

TO MANUFACTURE VICTORY

The preparation for war and the conversion of U.S. industry to war production was the single most important factor in the winning of World War II. In order to train the hundreds of thousands of pilots needed to fight the air war, the United States built more than 780 airports, complete with lodging for the pilots and hangars—large buildings for housing and repairing aircraft. Construction of manufacturing and training facilities alone involved millions of cubic yards of concrete and billions of feet of lumber. Before and during the war, between 18 and 40 million people held jobs in wartime and related industries. Such a huge workforce, all operating toward a common goal, had never been seen before. Without this effort, the nation's fighting forces would never have left U.S. shores and the Allies would not have had the weapons, equipment, and supplies needed to win the war.

Manufacturers produced everything the soldiers needed, from trucks to socks to aircraft and from pup tents to canned milk to ammunition. And manufacturers had to make everything just right. If the cans weren't perfect, food would spoil. If the ammunition wasn't perfect, weapons would jam. U.S. industry rose to the challenge with great results.

Here is just a portion of what the U.S. Army purchased to equip its troops during the war:

Tanks	88,410
Other combat vehicles	160,673
Heavy trucks (2.5 to 20 tons)	965,948
Heavy bombers (B-17, B-24)	34,780
Fighter planes	68,712
Machine guns	2.7 million
Rifles	6.6 million
Binoculars	781,065
Artillery and tank ammunition	300 million rounds
.50-caliber machine gun ammunition	10.5 billion rounds
.30-caliber ammunition	25.5 billion rounds
500-pound bombs	7.3 million
Incendiary bombs	5.3 million
Socks	519 million pairs
Foot powder	28.8 million cans
Pup tents	25 million
Ponchos and raincoats	38 million
Canned food	13.5 billion pounds
Radio sets	1.5 million

A U.S. pilot shoots down a German Messerschmitt *(background)* during a "dogfight," or air battle. The dark tail of the U.S. P-51 Mustang *(front)* shows that it is piloted by a Tuskegee Airman, or African American pilot.

The Eighth Air Force grew steadily, and the Army Air Forces managed to train far more pilots than were killed. In contrast, German pilots were killed at a high rate, and replacements had to be rushed in with little training. By mid-1943, the average German fighter pilot had fewer than 170 hours of training. U.S. pilots arrived in England with a minimum of 360 hours of training.

The Allies knew that if fighter planes could escort bombers and attack German fighters, bomber survival would improve and more Germans would be shot down. The United States accomplished this with the introduction of the P-51 fighter in November 1943. Fighter escorts became commonplace by early 1944. Bomber dam-age decreased, which meant less repair time and more bombers available for each raid.

U.S. AIRPOWER

Before the Allied invasion of Italy, U.S. B-24s had to fly from North Africa to bomb targets in Italy, the Balkans, and Austria. By late 1943, U.S. bombers could use airfields in southern Italy. From there, the bombers could reach well into Germany and also to oil fields in Romania. This freed up aircraft in England to support Eisenhower in preparation for the invasion of France. Starting in March 1944, the Allies intensified bombing of German-controlled bridges, roads, and rail yards in France. German units, particularly panzer and other units easily spotted from the air, suffered heavy losses. By the time of the invasion of France in June, Allied bombing had nearly paralyzed German transportation in France and had destroyed most of Germany's fighters there. The United States ruled the air and bombed at will. The Luftwaffe could do nothing to stop them.

After the invasion, the aircraft based in England went back to bombing targets in Germany. In July and August 1944, U.S. attacks on German oil fields, refineries, and synthetic oil plants created havoc. Germany's high-octane fuel production dropped from 150,000 tons in April 1944 to 5,000 tons in September. Synthetic fuel production went from more than 300,000 tons to less than 20,000 tons in September. As fuel reserves were used up, Germany slowed to a halt.

The Luftwaffe had so little aviation fuel that it cut pilot training first to 110 hours, then to 50 hours. With so little training, German pilots performed poorly. By August 1944, the average German pilot survived less then 30 days in combat. Albert Speer, Hitler's minister of armaments, managed to increase German weapons production in 1944, but it didn't make much difference. With so little fuel, troops couldn't use their new equipment. Speer had hundreds of new tanks ready for the Battle of the Bulge in December 1944. But the German attack plans depended on capturing Allied fuel reserves to power these tanks.

Attacks on synthetic fuel plants paid off for the Allies in another way. These attacks greatly reduced production of nitrogen and methanol, used in making explosives. Explosives were so short by late 1944 that German manufacturers added salt to artillery shells because there weren't enough pure explosives to fill the shells.

In an attempt to stop the bombing, Hitler pulled men and equipment from his eastern and western fronts. He assigned two million German soldiers to the antiaircraft defense of Germany. They used 20 percent of the nation's ammunition, 33 percent of its optical equipment, and 50 percent of its electronic equipment. By late 1944, nearly 75 percent of Germany's 88mm guns—the most fearsome antitank gun of all—were being used to shoot at bombers, even though German troops at the frontlines desperately needed these guns to fight U.S. and Soviet tanks.

In 1945 air attacks on Germany increased still further. In fact, more than 23 percent of all bombs dropped on Germany in the war fell between January 1 and May 4, 1945. The German economy lay in ruins. German armies and equipment couldn't move. The Luftwaffe was virtually nonexistent. The air forces of the United States had done it.

EYEWITNESS QUOTE:
THE NORMANDY SKY

"On June 11, 1944 . . . we were flying top cover . . . when there was a loud crack and pieces of shrapnel flew back into my cockpit. . . . I saw damage to the wing. Just then my element leader shouted on the radio, 'Herbie, there's a German on your tail!'"

—U.S. Thunderbolt fighter pilot "Lil' Herbie" Stachler

THE PLAN:
FORCED ENTRY

General Eisenhower's orders from the CCS were simple: "You will enter the continent of Europe and, in conjunction with other united nations, undertake operations aimed at the heart of Germany and the destruction of her armed forces." What a huge job such a simple mission statement actually demanded.

After the Cairo-Tehran conferences, Eisenhower's headquarters in Britain, Supreme Headquarters, Allied Expeditionary Force (SHAEF), completed the planning for Operation Overlord—the invasion of France. Eisenhower's staff selected France's Normandy region (100 miles south of Great Britain) as the invasion area.

Eisenhower commanded 2,876,000 men from more than a dozen countries. Each army had different training and used different weapons, radio frequencies, and methods of supply. Even if everybody liked each other (which they didn't), keeping this group together and having them fight as a coordinated team would prove incredibly difficult.

GERMAN CONFUSION

Eisenhower created a deception plan that included an entire fake army based north of London. Ideally positioned to land at Calais in northern France, the fake army included dummy tanks and trucks (some made from wood and canvas, others of inflatable rubber) and sent fake radio messages. Eisenhower pulled George Patton from retirement and made him commander of the fake army. The trick fooled the Germans. Even after Overlord began, many Germans, including Hitler, thought the main landing would come near Calais.

For his part, Hitler recalled Gerd von Rundstedt from retirement and named him commander west, responsible for the defense of France. Hitler kept some units under his personal command, however. He also gave Erwin Rommel command of an army group separate from Rundstedt. The Germans were well prepared for an invasion. They had created Festung Europa (Fortress Europe), a network of tens of thousands of pillboxes (gun emplacements), tank traps, and concrete artillery positions along the French coast. German fortified military posts plus the reserves in the rear totaled more than two million soldiers. Any invasion would meet stiff resistance.

> ### EYEWITNESS QUOTE: A GENERAL'S MESSAGE
>
> "I have full confidence in your courage, devotion to duty and skill in battle. We will accept nothing less than full victory."
>
> —General Dwight D. Eisenhower, on the invasion of Normandy

A German pillbox, or bunker with heavy artillery, faces the beach near Normandy, France. Thousands of pillboxes lined the coastline of France as part of Festung Europa, the German defense.

Organization and Rank, U.S. Infantry

Unit	Made Up Of	Commanded By
squad	ten men	staff sergeant
line platoon	three frontline squads and a weapons squad (with light machine guns and bazookas)	lieutenant
company	three frontline platoons, a weapons platoon (with heavy machine guns and mortars), and a headquarters (with supply trucks and a water trailer)	captain
battalion	three frontline companies, a weapons company (with mortars and antitank weapons), and a headquarters (supply) company	lieutenant colonel
regiment	three frontline battalions, a battalion-sized artillery and weapons unit, and a battalion-sized supply and service unit	colonel
division three	frontline regiments, a regimental-sized artillery, a regimental-sized supply and service unit (including engineers and medical staff), and a headquarters	major general
corps	two to five divisions, plus dozens of tank, artillery, antitank, engineering, antiaircraft, maintenance, supply, truck, fuel depot, ammunitions depot, and other regimental- and battalion-sized units	lieutenant general
army	two to four corps, plus dozens of extra and/or specialized regiments and battalions	general
army group	two to four armies, plus extra and specialized units, including harbor construction, longshoremen, railroad construction, railroad operation, fuel pipeline, and other supply-related regiments and battalions	general
expeditionary force (or theater)	two or more army groups	general

Eisenhower's D-Day Decision

To cross the English Channel safely, drop paratroopers, and land on the beaches of Normandy, the Allied Expeditionary Force needed a half-moon for light at night followed by a rising tide to help float landing craft to shore in the morning. This combination would occur twice in June— on June 5, 6, and 7 and then on June 19 and 20. General Dwight Eisenhower picked June 5 as the day for the invasion. After the first three sunny days of June, however, a terrible storm arrived on June 4. After talking with his staff, Eisenhower decided to postpone the invasion until June 6.

U.S. troops await their "go" orders for the invasion of Normandy.

For the soldiers in boats on the English Channel and for paratroopers at airfields in southern England, it was a long and miserable wait. The storm continued throughout the day of June 4. Eisenhower knew that if the weather did not improve in a few hours, he would have to postpone D-Day. Just as he was about to call off the invasion, aides handed him a weather report that predicted a slight break in the storm for the night of June 5 and the morning of June 6. After sleeping for a few hours, Eisenhower met with his staff again in the early morning hours of June 5. With the storm still raging, aides again told Eisenhower that the weather was expected to improve for a short time in the next 24 hours.

Should they go for D-Day or not? The decision was Eisenhower's alone to make. The general paced back and forth across a small room as the other officers looked on. Finally, he stopped pacing and looked at his men. Quietly and clearly, he said, "OK, let's go." The invasion was on. D-Day had an actual date: June 6, 1944.

OPERATION OVERLORD

The Allies divided the landing area at Normandy into five beaches: Sword, Gold, Juno, Omaha, and Utah. Each beach would be hit by only one nation's soldiers. The British would land at Sword and Gold, the Canadians at Juno, and the U.S. forces at Omaha and Utah. One infantry division would attack each beach.

Six infantry and two armored divisions stood by for immediate follow-up landings. Two U.S. airborne (paratrooper) divisions, the 82nd and the 101st, would jump in behind Utah Beach, and one British airborne division would jump in behind Sword. Carefully weighing the tides and weather, Eisenhower made the decision. The first day of the invasion, D-Day, would be June 6, 1944.

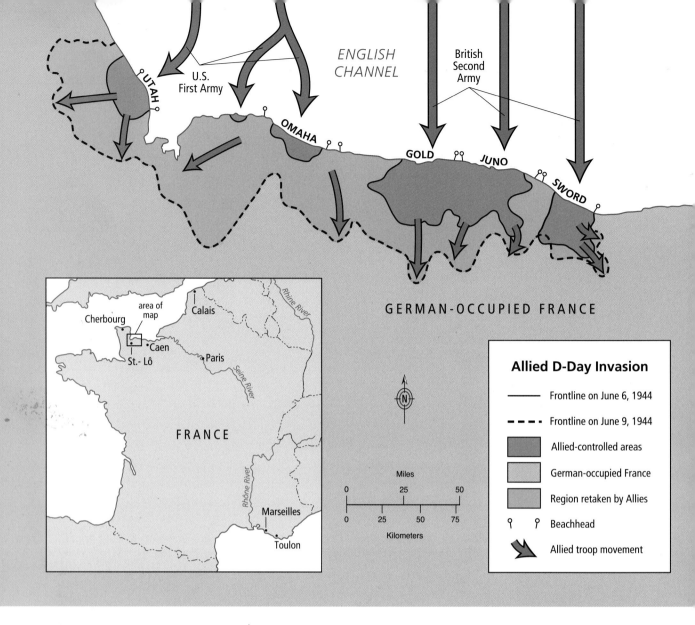

ENGLISH CHANNEL

British Second Army

U.S. First Army

UTAH

OMAHA

GOLD

JUNO

SWORD

GERMAN-OCCUPIED FRANCE

Allied D-Day Invasion

——— Frontline on June 6, 1944

- - - - Frontline on June 9, 1944

Allied-controlled areas

German-occupied France

Region retaken by Allies

Beachhead

Allied troop movement

Miles
0   25   50

0   25   50   75
Kilometers

area of map

Calais

Rhine River

Cherbourg

•Caen

St.- Lô

•Paris

Seine River

FRANCE

Rhône River

Marseilles

Toulon

N

Paratroopers began to jump at 1 A.M. on June 6. Though outnumbered, outgunned, and badly scattered, they fought hard, capturing and defending bridges and road junctions to keep German reinforcements from reaching Utah Beach. The airborne assault also caused great confusion in various German headquarters. The Germans couldn't figure out what was happening or how to react.

Seaborne infantry began to land at 6:30 A.M. The U.S. 4th Infantry Division came ashore at Utah, though wind and waves pushed them a mile from their designated landing zones. Once they stormed ashore, they changed plans as necessary. By the end of the day, they had established their beachhead—or secured territory along the shoreline—up to six miles deep.

Things didn't go as well at Omaha Beach. The first wave of U.S. infantry (two battalions) made their landing in the teeth of eight German battalions. The United States suffered high casualties in bitter and confused fighting. By the end of the day, more troops had landed, some organization had been restored, and the United States managed to push the beachhead a mile and a half inland.

At Sword, Gold, and Juno, British and Canadian forces met lighter resistance. But the British, under command of Bernard Montgomery, moved more slowly than U.S. forces. The British failed to seize the first day's most important objective: the city of Caen, France.

**EYEWITNESS QUOTE:
THE SHORES OF NORMANDY**

"Machine gun fire hit around the . . . boat. . . . When the ramp went down we started for the obstacles. A [shell] exploded near my feet. Had I not been flattened out, the shrapnel . . . would have probably killed me."

—Sergeant Roy Arnn

THE GERMANS REACT

Starting at 2 A.M. on June 6, Rundstedt alerted many reserve units to prepare to move and fight. But the units that Hitler controlled did not receive any orders from him and ignored Rundstedt. Rommel was in Germany for his wife's birthday party, and his army group ignored Rundstedt too. German command sent more orders later in the day, but many reserve units didn't actually start moving until late afternoon on June 6 or the morning of June 7.

Allied troops take cover behind tank barriers as they fight their way onto Omaha Beach. Tired, cold, and seasick, Allied soldiers faced rough tide, tricky obstacles, and a barrage of German machine gun and artillery fire. Many did not make it to the beach alive.

MEDICAL CARE UNDER FIRE

All U.S. military divisions had a medical battalion. This unit included field hospitals near battle sites, ambulances, nurses, and medics. Medics were unarmed soldiers, trained and equipped for advanced first aid, who traveled with the fighting troops. During battle, medics treated wounded soldiers where they fell and then transported them back to field hospitals. If his wounds were serious enough, a soldier would be moved to a larger and more capable field hospital farther to the rear. If necessary, he would be put on a hospital ship and sent back to the United States for more medical care.

Nurses (generally women) worked in field hospitals and hospital ships, right behind the fighting soldiers and sailors. Military nurses underwent field training much like male soldiers, and many lived like infantrymen, sleeping in tents clustered around field hospitals. The Navy Nurse Corps numbered more than 11,000, and the Army Nurse Corps was 55,000 strong.

Medics wore helmets or armbands marked with red crosses, and all ambulances and field hospital tents were also marked with red crosses. Though most armies did not intentionally fire upon medical personnel, hundreds of medics, and even doctors and nurses in field hospitals, were killed during the war. At Anzio in Italy, for instance, six nurses were killed when their field hospital was bombed. Despite these losses and the loss of the hospital's electric generators, the doctors and nurses at Anzio kept working, performing surgery by flashlight.

In war, soldiers die from illness as well as combat wounds. A drug called penicillin, discovered by British scientist Alexander Fleming in 1928, was used to keep bacteria from growing in open wounds and to control diseases such as pneumonia. Thanks to penicillin, only 0.5 percent of the soldiers who got pneumonia during World War II died from the disease. In World War I, before the discovery of penicillin, pneumonia killed nearly one out of every four soldiers who developed the disease.

U.S. medics treat a fallen infantryman during the Allied invasion of France in 1944.

Movement in daylight was a bad idea. Allied fighters attacked anything they could see. They pounded Fritz Bayerlein's Panzer Lehr Division as it tried to move to Normandy. The attacks forced Bayerlein to leap from his car and take cover in ditches more than a dozen times on June 8 alone. Finally, his car was destroyed and his driver killed. Many Germans tore the doors off their cars and trucks so they could get out faster when Allied planes attacked. German reinforcements began arriving in Normandy on the night of June 8. Despite heavy casualties from aerial attacks, the defending Germans fought well. Panzer Lehr stopped a British attack on Caen on June 13.

The Allies faced supply problems. They built two artificial harbors (one British and one U.S.), so that oceangoing ships could unload gasoline, ammunition, and food directly across the landing beaches. But storms wrecked the U.S. harbor. Despite stiff German resistance, lack of supplies, and marshy terrain beyond Omaha and Utah Beaches, the U.S. forces had pushed across the Normandy Peninsula by June 18. They captured the city of Cherbourg on June 27.

A Final Resting Place

The World War II Normandy American Cemetery and Memorial sits on the bluff overlooking Omaha Beach. The cemetery holds the graves of more than 9,300 U.S. soldiers who died during the invasion of Europe and is the site of a monument for the more than 1,500 U.S. soldiers whose bodies were never found. After the war, many citizens of Normandy volunteered to put flowers on the graves of their U.S. "sons." The American Battle Monuments Commission maintains U.S. military cemeteries and monuments on foreign soil, including the cemetery in Normandy. You can visit the monument commission's website at <www.abmc.gov>.

German prisoners of war march through Cherbourg, France, under U.S. escort following intense fighting for the city in June 1944. Capturing the coastal town meant that the Allies had a port from which to supply the advancing attack across France. Before this could happen, however, the U.S. Army Corps of Engineers had to clear the harbor of German mines.

British troops stand in the war-torn streets of Caen, France, during the Allied advance in the summer of 1944. A road sign points the way to Paris, the route of the Allied campaign.

By June 30, Rundstedt realized that he couldn't stop the U.S. forces. He telephoned Hitler's headquarters, yelling "Make peace, you idiots!" Refusing to listen, on July 2, Hitler had Field Marshal Hans Günther von Kluge flown in from the eastern front to replace Rundstedt. By July 18, the U.S. troops had fought their way through thick hedgerow country to take the city of Saint-Lô, France. They were on the verge of breaking out into open country. On July 20, the British finally took Caen.

On that same day, Hitler survived an assassination attempt by a German officer. Hitler began merciless killings of anyone he suspected of helping or even knowing about the attempt. General after general was either executed or forced to commit suicide. No one was safe. Even Erwin Rommel, recovering from wounds received in a fighter attack on his car, was suspected of having heard about the attempt. Hitler gave Rommel a choice: either Hitler's police would seize Rommel's wife, family, friends, and staff and torture them to death, or Rommel could commit suicide. Rommel chose suicide by poison.

PATTON REDEEMED

Bayerlein's Panzer Lehr Division moved opposite Saint-Lô. But its positions were exactly where General Omar Bradley, the commander of the U.S. land forces, wanted to attack. On July 25, the Eighth Air Force dropped 4,200 tons of bombs on Panzer Lehr, and the U.S. forces surged forward. A staff officer presented orders to Bayerlein:

not a single man was to leave his position. Bayerlein furiously replied, "Not a single man is leaving his post . . . for they are dead." On July 27, a German staff officer removed the Panzer Lehr marker from the map at Hitler's headquarters—Panzer Lehr had ceased to exist. By then the U.S. troops had penetrated more than 10 miles into the German lines. The city of Avranches, France, fell on July 30. A hole had been torn in the German defense.

Eisenhower decided to give General Patton a second chance, putting him in charge of the Third Army under Bradley. Patton's troops plunged through the hole in the German lines at Avranches and advanced 80 miles in two days. By August 8, Patton had seized the Brittany Peninsula to the southwest of Normandy and reached the city of Le Mans, France, to the east. He then wheeled some of his divisions north toward the British at Caen. If he moved fast enough, he and the British could cut off almost all the defending Germans, trapping more than 200,000 of them.

On August 13, Patton reached the boundary between the U.S. and British forces. But Montgomery didn't react to the opportunity that lay before him. On August 19, he sent the Free Polish Brigade to link up with Patton, but it was too late. Most of the Germans had escaped the trap that Patton had laid.

Patton wouldn't stand still. He attacked east toward Paris, the French capital, with two of his corps. Knowing that the U.S. forces were coming, the Free French rose up in Paris and began fighting the Germans in the streets. Shifting his units so that the Free French 2nd Armored Division led the

way, Patton moved into Paris. By August 25, the city was free and Patton had reached the upper waters of the Seine River. While Patton's soldiers covered 170 miles, Montgomery and the British moved barely 20 and still had not reached the mouth of the Seine.

As Patton charged across France, the United States, assisted by the Free French, launched another invasion. The U.S. Seventh Army and the Free French First Army landed in the south of France on August 15. By August 28, they had captured the French port cities of Toulon and Marseilles and advanced 150 miles up the Rhone Valley.

Victorious U.S. troops march along the Champs Elysées, a boulevard in Paris, fast on the heels of retreating German forces in August 1944.

Blood Supply and the Blood Line

Dr. Charles Drew, a surgeon at Columbia University, experimented in the 1930s with the problem of storing blood safely. In World War I, many wounded soldiers had died because blood spoiled so fast (in just a week) that doctors didn't have enough usable blood on hand. Drew discovered that blood plasma (the liquid part of blood) could be stored far longer than whole blood (plasma and blood cells together).

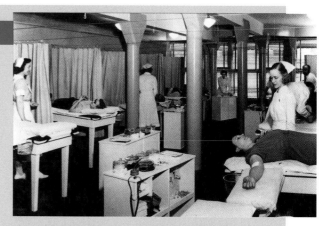

U.S. citizens donate blood to the war effort at a blood bank in the 1940s.

Thanks to his work, Drew was named medical supervisor of the Blood for Britain program during World War II. He taught staff at U.S. hospitals how to separate plasma from whole blood and to store it safely. He then supervised shipment of blood supplies from the United States to Britain, where the blood was used to treat wounded Allied soldiers.

Also in the 1930s, Frederick McKinley Jones invented refrigeration equipment for transporting perishable goods. During the war, his Thermo King Corporation made refrigeration units for carrying blood plasma to Allied troops in combat.

It is ironic that Jones and Drew were responsible for getting plasma where it was needed to save lives—because both men were African American. During the war, U.S. society and the military were so rigidly segregated that "colored blood" was kept separate from "white blood." White soldiers couldn't receive blood or plasma donated by African Americans.

SUPPLY PROBLEMS

On September 4, Hitler recalled Rundstedt and made him commander in the west once again. Even though the Germans had escaped Patton's trap, U.S. airpower and slashing ground attacks had nearly destroyed the German Fifth Panzer and Seventh Armies. Only 120 German tanks remained to oppose Montgomery and Bradley with their thousands of tanks. Rundstedt and Guderian, by then recalled from retirement and made chief of the army staff, laid plans to bring in reinforce-ments and fight again. But they needed time. Allied supply problems, worsened by British delays, would give it to them.

Each U.S. army needed 400,000 gallons of gasoline, or a full shipload, every three days. And the gasoline had to be delivered to each vehicle, no matter what field or woods that vehicle was crossing. Each tank or artillery piece could fire a ton of ammu-nition in a day, and that ammunition needed to be constantly replaced. Every sol-dier needed food and ammunition, no mat-ter where he was. Someone had to unload all this material from ships, transport it to the front, and deliver it. In July and August, the only operational Allied ports in France were at Cherbourg and Grandville. They weren't able to fully supply everyone.

Montgomery demanded the majority of available supplies for his troops so he could take another port, Antwerp in Belgium. Determined to keep the coalition together, Eisenhower gave him the supplies he asked for. The British captured Antwerp on September 4. But they couldn't use the port because the Germans still held the Schelde Estuary, the shipway to the docks.

Montgomery continued to demand supply priority. He went around Eisenhower to the BCS, promising that he could make one bold thrust into Germany and end the war. He planned to use U.S. and British paratroopers to capture bridges across all the rivers in Belgium and the Netherlands. Then he would push his XXX Armored Corps across these bridges and into Germany. Roosevelt was friendly with Churchill, and the JCS wanted to keep both Roosevelt and Churchill happy. They pressured Eisenhower to approve the attack, known as Operation Market-Garden.

Allied aircraft drop thousands of paratroopers behind enemy lines in the Netherlands in 1944. The plan, called Operation Market-Garden, was to secure routes to Germany through the Netherlands and Belgium.

Montgomery launched Market-Garden on September 17, 1944. U.S. forces seized the bridges they were supposed to, but the British failed to take theirs at Arnhem in the Netherlands. The XXX Armored Corps moved slowly, hemmed in by the terrain. By September 25, the British were stopped. Their paratroopers had either surrendered or retreated.

The U.S. forces worked frantically to solve supply issues. Troops rebuilt French railways and bridges, laid gasoline pipelines, and opened the ports of Le Havre and Rouen to shipping. Finally, Montgomery also turned his attention to the ports. He ordered Canadian troops to attack the Schelde Estuary. They succeeded, and the first Allied ship docked in Antwerp on November 28. But by the time adequate supplies started flowing to Bradley, the Germans had rebuilt the Fifth Panzer and Seventh Armies.

POISED FOR ATTACK

On September 11, the Allies advancing from Marseilles, under command of U.S. general Jacob Devers, had linked up with General Bradley. Bradley and Devers faced Germany, creating a solid Allied line from Switzerland to the ocean. Those Germans left in France were behind enemy lines.

On December 7, 1944, General Eisenhower ordered the offensive of 1945. Montgomery and Bradley would attack, capture Germany's industrial Ruhr region, then continue to Berlin. Devers would make a secondary attack. U.S. troops stood poised on the German frontier. But they faced tough fighting and the worst winter weather in Europe in 40 years.

American soldiers build a bridge across a river in France. The Germans destroyed bridges to slow Allied progress toward Germany.

A SHORT ONE THOUSAND YEARS

9

As Eisenhower prepared his attack, Hitler planned an offensive of his own. He would attack through the Ardennes Forest, cutting off and destroying all Allied forces north of his anticipated breakthrough. Rundstedt and Guderian readied their forces.

Due to bad weather and bad information gathering, Allied intelligence troops didn't see the German concentration of forces. On December 16, 1944, the German Sixth Panzer, Fifth Panzer, and Seventh Armies launched their attack. By luck, they fell upon the area of General Courtney Hodges's First Army that was most thinly held. Only the 14th Cavalry Regiment and the 28th and 106th Infantry Divisions stood in the Germans' way.

The Germans wanted to attack under the cover of bad weather. They got their wish. Under cover of fog, clouds, and snow, the Germans pushed aside the 14th and slashed into the 106th. The next day, two regiments of the 106th, cut off by the Germans, surrendered. The 28th withdrew in one piece.

Reports streamed into SHAEF. Eisenhower realized this was a major attack. German forces had pushed into the Ally-held frontline, creating a bulge in it. (The fight to push back the Germans would come to be called the Battle of the Bulge.) Eisenhower ordered the 7th Armored Division, the 10th Armored Division, and the entire U.S. airborne (rebuilt after the Operation Market-Garden disaster) to the Ardennes.

The Ardennes

Thinking the Ardennes Forest was the least likely spot for a German offensive, the U.S. troops were thinly spread there along the German border. But the Germans attacked at 5:30 A.M. on December 16, along an 84-mile front from Monschau, Germany, in the north to Echternach, Luxembourg, in the south. After four days of fighting, the Germans had pushed back the U.S. forces, creating a wedge, or bulge, in the U.S. line about 30 miles deep. By Christmas Eve, the Germans had made their farthest advance, nearly 50 miles deep, almost to the Meuse River in Belgium. Four weeks later, after grim fighting and with heavy losses on both sides, the opposing armies stood at their former positions. The Bulge ceased to exist.

U.S. infantrymen in the Ardennes Forest

The 7th went to Saint-Vith, Belgium, while the 101st Airborne and part of the 10th went to Bastogne, Belgium, both important road junctions. Deep snow on the ground would keep much of the German forces on the road, so road junctions were critical.

Though badly outnumbered and hopelessly outgunned, the 101st Airborne fought defiantly. The Germans cut them off and surrounded the city of Bastogne on December 21. The Germans demanded that the 101st surrender or be annihilated. Anthony McAuliff, commander of the 101st, answered with one word: "Nuts!" The Germans never took Bastogne.

> ### EYEWITNESS QUOTE: THE 761ST TANK BATTALION AND THE ARDENNES
>
> "Well I don't know what day it is because we have been so busy fighting. . . . A lot of my buddies have been killed here but . . . I am still here. We have taken a beating but these guys are still pitching and whoever said 'the colored soldier can't fight' is a . . . liar. The guys in the infantry told us they'd rather have us with them than the white soldiers."
>
> —Staff Sergeant Johnnie Stevens, 761st Tank Battalion, 1944

Across the battle area, U.S. units used their own initiative to fight the Germans.

The German plan relied on their capturing U.S. fuel supplies. But not a drop of gasoline fell into German hands. The German drive began to slow.

At a meeting at Verdun, France, on December 19, Eisenhower had said that he wanted to counterattack quickly. Patton stated that he could attack on December 22. Nobody believed he could move so fast. Eisenhower ordered attacks to begin on the 23rd or 24th. Bradley couldn't move his army group headquarters to a position with good communication and transportation abilities. So Eisenhower changed the command boundary. Montgomery would handle everything on the north side of the Bulge, and Bradley the south side. This decision, effective December 20, placed the U.S. Ninth Army and most of the First Army under Montgomery's command.

THE BATTLE FOR BASTOGNE

George Patton shone in one of his finest hours. Using masterful staff work, he pulled two corps (more than 50,000 men and 8,000 vehicles) out of line, moved them 50 miles to the north, and attacked toward Bastogne on December 22. The weather cleared on December 23, allowing U.S. air forces to pound Germans locations. On December 25, elements of the U.S. 2nd and 9th Armored Divisions

stopped the German advance short of the Meuse River.

The Americans saw the battle as a tremendous opportunity. If they did it right, they could cut off and destroy the three German armies. That would leave no one to stop an attack into Germany. But then Montgomery ordered the U.S. units under his command to retreat. He insisted that the Bulge could never be turned into a victory. He again bypassed his superior, Eisenhower, and sent messages directly to Churchill and the BCS. He said that the U.S. forces were defeated, outmatched, and confused.

Not knowing that he was supposed to be defeated, outmatched, and confused, Patton punched through to Bastogne on December 26. He continued to attack the Bulge from the south to cut off the Germans.

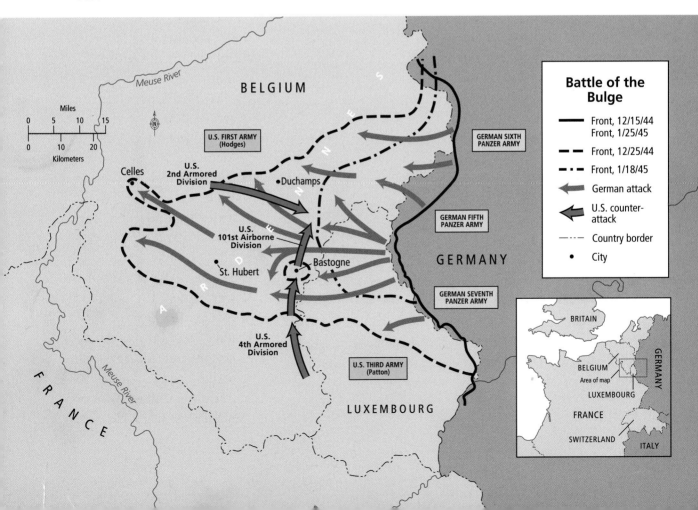

But no attack came from Montgomery in the north. It began to look like a repeat of the earlier trap near Caen that Patton had set and Montgomery had failed to close.

Fed up with Montgomery, Eisenhower prepared to relieve him of command. Montgomery finally got the message and attacked on January 3, 1945. He linked up with Patton on January 16, but the Germans withdrew before the Allies could cut them off.

THE BRIDGE AT REMAGEN

The Allies had been stalled at the German border long enough for the Germans to rebuild their border defenses, called the Siegfried Line, or West Wall. Eisenhower ordered Bradley, Devers and Montgomery, to bust through the Siegfried Line, advance to the Rhine River, and cross the Rhine into Germany.

The offensive started in Montgomery's area on February 8, 1945. In 15 days, Montgomery gained only about 15 miles. On February 23, he allowed the U.S. Ninth Army to attack. In only 11 days, it penetrated the line and got to the Rhine. The Germans were disorganized, so the commander of the Ninth Army proposed an immediate attack across the Rhine. Montgomery refused.

Bradley's First Army attacked the Siegfried Line on February 23, broke through on March 5, and got to the Rhine in two days. His 9th Armored Division moved fast, reaching the German town of Remagen and

U.S. forces cross Ludendorff Bridge at Remagen, Germany, in February 1945. U.S. general William Hoge, defying orders, sent an infantry battalion and two armored divisions to capture the prized bridge. The U.S. forces won the race to cross the Rhine before retreating Germans could destroy the span. Ludendorff Bridge collapsed on March 17, after thousands of troops and supplies had crossed on the way to Berlin.

Liberation of the Camps

As the Allies closed in on Germany, they discovered the horror of the death camps. Soviet troops advanced westward from the east and were the first to see the camps, including Maidanek and Auschwitz in Poland. They found few Jewish prisoners to free, because the Nazis had increased the killing of the prisoners or forced them to western camps as the Allies neared.

U.S. and British troops moving in from the west liberated Bergen-Belsen, Dachau *(right)*, and Mauthausen in Germany. Many more surviving Jews were in these camps. But the soldiers quickly learned of the millions who had been murdered, the evidence of which was to be found in mass graves and in the surrounding fields covered in human ashes.

seizing a bridge across the Rhine before the Germans could blow it up. Bradley immediately sent more units to the bridgehead (the secured territory around the bridge).

Patton had already made two penetrations of the Siegfried Line. When he launched his next attack on March 13, he broke through immediately. He cut behind the German Seventh Army, determined that they would not escape him again. He got to the Rhine before the Germans could retreat and linked up with the 6th Army Group along the river. The surrounded German Seventh Army surrendered.

As the Allies moved in from the west, Hitler still had to fight the Soviets to the east. The Soviets had launched a general offensive on December 16, 1944. They seized Budapest, Hungary, on February 13, 1945, and Vienna, Austria, on April 13.

They also attacked in Poland, but the Germans stopped them at the Oder River, 40 miles short of Berlin.

While cutting off the German Seventh Army, Patton brought bridging forces (assault boats, pontoon bridges, and engineers) behind his attacking divisions. In a surprise move, he attacked across the Rhine at Oppenheim on March 22. Within two days, he had four divisions across the Rhine in a secure bridgehead. He also forced a crossing at Boppard on March 24, 1945. That gave Eisenhower three bridgeheads across the Rhine, all in the 12th Army Group's area.

Montgomery attacked across the Rhine on March 23. Unlike Patton's fast, surprise crossing, Montgomery needed heavy bombers, 3,300 artillery pieces, and an airborne (paratrooper) drop of two divisions, but he also successfully crossed the river. Patton attacked from his two bridgeheads on March 25. In three days, he was 70 miles deep into Germany. The First Army, breaking through at Remagen, was not far behind.

On March 28, Eisenhower issued new orders. Montgomery would encircle the Ruhr area from the north, while Bradley encircled it from the south. With the encirclement complete, the U.S. Ninth Army would go back to Bradley's control. Bradley would then attack across Germany to Dresden. Eisenhower ordered Devers to attack through southern Germany toward Vienna. The Ruhr was cut off on April 4.

The Ninth Army went back to Bradley. The unstoppable advance of U.S. forces picked up speed.

In April the Allies advanced on Germany from every direction. The Soviets attacked from the east, across the Oder River, surrounding Berlin. Montgomery came from the north, reaching the North Sea, and other British troops reached the Baltic Sea to the northeast of Germany. Patton crossed the Czech frontier to the east, and Devers's 6th Army Group took Munich. Other U.S. troops came from the south, charging across northern Italy to the Austrian border.

(From left to right, seated) **The "Big Three"—Winston Churchill, Franklin Delano Roosevelt, and Joseph Stalin—during the Yalta conference. The three Allied leaders met in 1945 to discuss how to rebuild postwar Europe.**

Allied Occupation Zones in Germany 1945

NORTH SEA

BALTIC SEA

EAST PRUSSIA

U.S. Zone

British Zone

Berlin (Allied)

POLAND

G E R M A N Y

Soviet Zone

NETHERLANDS

BELGIUM

LUXEMBOURG

FRANCE

French Zone

United States Zone

CZECHOSLOVAKIA

Soviet Zone

British Zone

SWITZERLAND

ITALY

YUGOSLAVIA

German border

Country border

Miles
0   50   100   150

0   100   200
Kilometers

Berlin Occupation Zones

French Zone

British Zone

Soviet Zone

U.S. Zone

Miles
0   2   4
0   2   6
Kilometers

THE END GAME

The final conference of the European war, attended by Roosevelt, Churchill, and Stalin, had been held in February 1945 at Yalta, a city on the Black Sea in modern-day Ukraine. Anticipating an Allied victory, the three leaders split Germany and Berlin into four "zones of occupation." Great Britain, France, the Soviet Union, and the United States would each control a zone. Each Allied nation would be responsible for administering its zone and providing services such as law enforcement, electricity, food, fuel, and governance.

Back in the battlefield, Allied soldiers raced across Germany toward Berlin. Along the way, they discovered dozens of prison camps and concentration camps, where 12 million people had perished and thousands remained imprisoned. U.S. soldiers freed and cared for the starving and brutalized camp inmates. When Eisenhower learned of the concentration camps, he became enraged. He ordered local German authorities to visit the camps to see the horror for themselves. He had camp employees, German prisoners of war, and German civilians bury the bodies of the dead.

Hitler's Fall

As the war dragged on and German armies were defeated in the Soviet Union and across Europe, Hitler's behavior and judgement became increasingly unpredictable and dangerous. Especially after the failed attempt on his life in July 1944, Hitler began to suspect enemies and traitors among even his most trusted aides. In the last year of the war, he made a great many blunders in military strategy, resulting in unnecessary losses among his troops and the German people.

By the spring of 1945, Hitler's armies were all but destroyed. The Soviets had almost complete control of Berlin. Along with his close friends and aides, Hitler lived in a bunker beneath the Reich Chancellery, his office building in Berlin. At 12:30 in the afternoon on April 30, 1945, with the Soviets only a block from the bunker, Hitler held his final staff conference. Berlin was no longer defensible. The end had come.

Hitler ate lunch with his two secretaries and his cook. Afterward, he and his new wife, Eva Braun, said good-bye to their colleagues, then retired to a private room. In a few moments, a shot rang out. Those outside waited for a second shot, but there was only silence. Then they quietly entered the room, where they found Hitler's body sprawled on a couch. He had shot himself. At his side lay Eva Braun, dead apparently from taking poison.

Hitler killed himself in April 1945, when he realized that Berlin was lost to advancing Soviet forces. In May the Soviets captured Berlin and raised their flag over the Reichstag, or German parliament building (above).

He also insisted that journalists write about this darkest of Nazi operations.

The war in Europe was near its end. The Soviets surrounded Berlin on April 25, and bitter fighting raged in the city for several days. Adolf Hitler committed suicide on April 30. The last holdouts in Berlin surrendered on May 2. Hitler's successor, Karl Doenitz, began negotiations with the Allies. He formally surrendered on May 7, 1945. Adolf Hitler had bragged that his Third Reich would last 1,000 years.

Accused of war crimes including the Holocaust, German military and government officials sit in the defendants' box *(center)* during the Nuremberg Trials in Germany.

After the German surrender, Eisenhower issued orders for his forces to withdraw to their nations' zones of occupation. As the U.S. forces moved to their zone, they encountered millions of refugees fleeing the Soviet zone. The U.S. troops rescued many of them, taking them to the U.S. zone on the backs of tanks.

The United States had not asked for World War II and did not start it. But the mightiest army in the world, backed by the finest air force in the world, supported by one of the greatest industrial economies the world had ever seen, helped to decisively finish it.

Punishing the Nazis

In 1945 and 1946, more than 20 Nazi leaders faced Allied judges at the International Military Tribunal (court) for crimes against humanity. The war crimes trials took place in Nuremberg, Germany. Most of the accused insisted that they were only following orders in carrying out the killings. Three of the accused were cleared. The rest were imprisoned or hanged, except for Hermann Goering. He committed suicide by swallowing cyanide—a form of the same poison that he had used to kill so many Jews.

EPILOGUE

At war's end, destruction and devastation lay across Europe. In all, more than 20 million private homes had been damaged or destroyed. Untold millions of other buildings, including factories, schools, and churches, lay in ruins. The rebuilding process took decades, with the last piles of rubble in Germany not cleared away until the 1970s.

More than the physical cost of the war, the human cost was staggering. The exact numbers will never be known, but the best estimates of military dead are about 20 million and civilian dead about 30 to 35 million. About the same numbers had been injured. Millions of Europeans became refugees—people who fled their homes to escape bombing or conquering armies. For a time, more than one million European refugees lived in temporary camps, run by international relief agencies, until they were able to return to their homes or find new ones. The Jews who had survived the Holocaust had no homes or families to return to and no desire to live among their former oppressors in Europe. Most Holocaust survivors moved to Israel, a new Jewish state established in 1948.

The American celebration of victory—called V-E (Victory in Europe) Day and held on May 8, 1945—was short. War still raged in the Pacific.

The United Nations

As soldiers from opposing nations attacked and killed one another in World War II, the world was also preparing for peace. At Tehran, Yalta, and other wartime conferences, Allied leaders discussed plans to establish an international organization, called the United Nations (UN), to help keep world peace once the war was over.

In 1945 representatives from 50 countries met in San Francisco, California, to draw up the UN Charter. The organization officially came into being on October 24, 1945. The UN focused on finding solutions to world disputes and economic, social, cultural, and humanitarian problems that can lead to war. The UN continues these efforts in the twenty-first century.

Though the mainland United States had not been bombed during the war, it had undergone major changes. Women had taken jobs outside the home. People of color had fought as equals and were determined to be treated as equals back in the United States. Household goods stayed in short supply for more than three years after the war, as U.S. industry switched back to civilian production. Most important, in just six short years, the United States had gone from sleepy isolationism to become the biggest economic and military power in the world.

Many people in the United States were descended from European immigrants and felt obligated to rebuild Europe after the war. What's more, the U.S. government knew that to keep Soviet Communism from spreading across Europe, war-torn nations would need economic and political stability. In 1947 U.S. Army chief of staff George Marshall became the U.S. secretary of state. He created a plan whereby the United States would provide money, industrial equipment, building materials, and other economic aid to Europe, including Germany. The Marshall Plan is credited with not only relieving human suffering but also with rebuilding many European nations as free, democratic countries.

At the dawn of the twenty-first century, all of the horrible destruction brought by World War II is behind us. The grass grows green across the former battlefields of Europe. It is broken only by the tombstones and the flowers above the graves of the dead.

MAJOR BATTLES OF WORLD WAR II IN EUROPE

German invasion of Poland	September 1, 1939
German invasion of Norway and Denmark	April 9, 1940
German invasion of Belgium, the Netherlands, and France	May 10, 1940
Battle of Britain	July to October 1940
German invasion of the Soviet Union	June 22, 1941
Battles for Kiev, Kursk, Leningrad, Moscow, Sevastopol, and Stalingrad	June 1941 to June 1944
The Japanese bomb Pearl Harbor, Hawaii (not on map)	December 7, 1941
Battle of El Alamein	October to November 1942
Allied invasion of Algeria and Morocco	November 8, 1942
Allied invasion of Tunisia and Libya	February to May 1943
Allied invasion of Sicily	July 10, 1943
Battle for Monte Cassino, Italy	January 4 to May 18, 1944
Allied invasion of Italy at Anzio	January 22, 1944
Allied invasion of France at Normandy (D-Day)	June 6, 1944
Allied invasion of southern France	August 1944
Battle of the Bulge in Belgium	December 1944

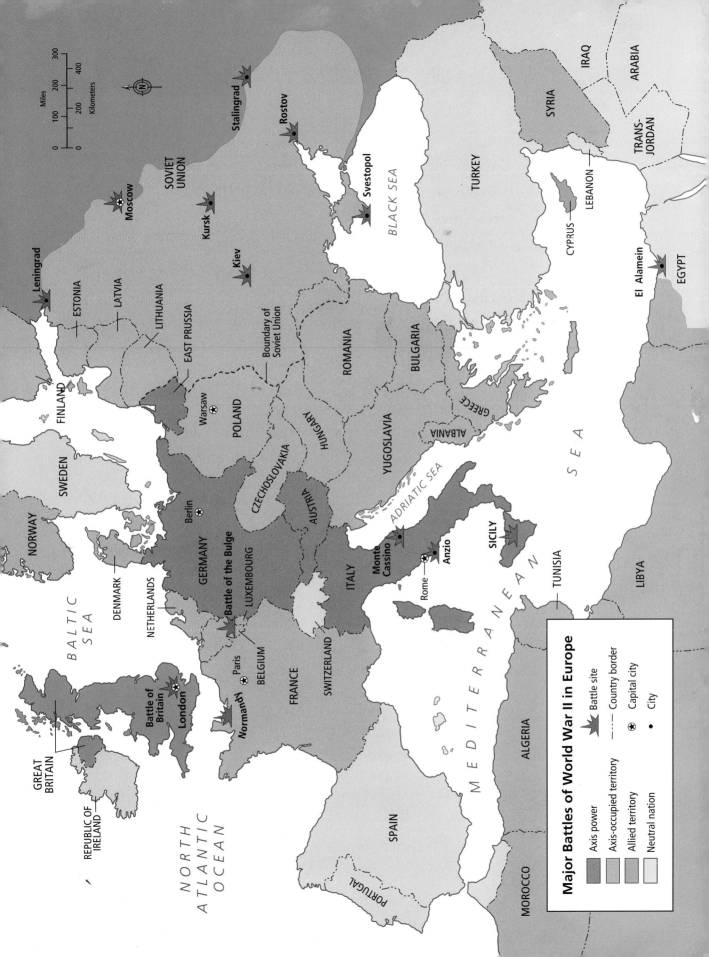

Major Battles of World War II in Europe

Battle site ![star]
Country border — · · —
Capital city ✪
City •

Axis power

Axis-occupied territory

Allied territory

Neutral nation

NORTH ATLANTIC OCEAN

GREAT BRITAIN

REPUBLIC OF IRELAND

Battle of Britain

London ✪

Battle of the Bulge

Normandy

Paris ✪

BELGIUM

FRANCE

SWITZERLAND

LUXEMBOURG

GERMANY

Berlin ✪

AUSTRIA

ITALY

Rome •

Anzio

Monte Cassino

SICILY

Battle of the Bulge

BALTIC SEA

NORWAY

SWEDEN

DENMARK

NETHERLANDS

FINLAND

ESTONIA

LATVIA

LITHUANIA

EAST PRUSSIA

Leningrad

Warsaw ✪

POLAND

CZECHOSLOVAKIA

HUNGARY

Boundary of Soviet Union

SOVIET UNION

Moscow ✪

Kursk

Kiev •

Stalingrad

Rostov

Svestopol

BLACK SEA

TURKEY

ROMANIA

BULGARIA

YUGOSLAVIA

ALBANIA

GREECE

ADRIATIC SEA

TUNISIA

LIBYA

ALGERIA

SPAIN

PORTUGAL

MOROCCO

MEDITERRANEAN SEA

CYPRUS

LEBANON

SYRIA

IRAQ

ARABIA

TRANS-JORDAN

EGYPT

El Alamein

Miles
300
200
100
0

Kilometers
400
200
0

WORLD WAR II IN EUROPE TIMELINE

January 30, 1933	Adolf Hitler becomes chancellor of Germany.
September 1, 1939	Germany invades Poland.
April 9, 1940	Germany invades Norway and Denmark.
May 10, 1940	Germany invades Belgium, the Netherlands, and France.
June 22, 1940	France signs an armistice with Germany.
September 16, 1940	The United States begins its first peacetime draft.
January 7, 1941	President Franklin Roosevelt signs an executive order establishing the U.S. Office of Production Management.
March 27, 1941	The lend-lease program begins. It allows the United States to provide weapons to its allies without immediate payment.
June 22, 1941	Germany invades the Soviet Union.
December 5, 1941	The Soviets stop the German offensive outside Moscow.
December 7, 1941	The Japanese bomb Pearl Harbor, Hawaii.
December 11, 1941	The United States declares war on Germany and Italy.
August 17, 1942	The United States makes its first bombing raid in Europe, targeting a German-held railroad yard in Rouen, France.
October 23, 1942	The Allies fight the Battle of El Alamein in Egypt.
November 8, 1942	The first U.S. troops invade North Africa.
February 2, 1943	German general Friedrich Paulus surrenders at Stalingrad, Soviet Union.
July 10, 1943	The Allies invade Sicily.
September 3, 1943	Italy surrenders to the Allies.
June 6, 1944	The Allies invade Normandy, France (D-Day).
July 25, 1944	U.S. forces break through the German line at Saint-Lô, France.
August 25, 1944	U.S. forces and the Free French liberate Paris.
December 22–26, 1944	U.S. forces stop the German attack and defend Bastogne, Belgium, in the Battle of the Bulge.
March 7, 1945	U.S. troops seize the Ludendorff bridge across the Rhine River at Remagen, Germany.
March 22, 1945	U.S forces make a surprise crossing of the Rhine River at Oppenheim, Germany.
March 25, 1945	U.S. forces launch a final attack into Germany.
April 30, 1945	Adolf Hitler commits suicide.
May 2, 1945	The Soviets seize Berlin.
May 4, 1945	U.S. forces in Germany and Italy link up near Brenner Pass (route between Italy and Austria).
May 7, 1945	Germany stops fighting and surrenders all forces, effective May 9, 1945.
May 8, 1945	President Harry S. Truman declares this day as the official Victory in Europe Day (V-E Day).

GLOSSARY

artillery: large weapons that fire explosive shells. Howitzers are a type of artillery.

beachhead: an area of enemy shoreline that has been taken under control by an invading army

blitzkrieg: war conducted with great speed and force, including the use of massive air attacks and moving ground forces

casualties: soldiers lost to an army due to death, injury, illness, or imprisonment by the enemy

civil defense: a system of protective measures undertaken by civilians in preparation for and warning of an enemy attack. Air-raid wardens, who spot incoming enemy aircraft and warn the public, are a form of civil defense.

coalition: a group of two or more nations that pledge to work together to achieve a common goal

Communism: a system in which the government controls the nation's economy, with no private property

convoy: a group of vehicles, such as ships, traveling close to each other and to a common destination

dictator: a ruler who has absolute power. Many dictators rule oppressively, using fear and brutality to make citizens obey their authority.

infantryman: a soldier who fights on foot. Infantrymen are usually armed with pistols, rifles, hand grenades, and machine guns.

isolationist: a person who wants his or her nation to stay out of foreign affairs and foreign alliances

neutrality: refusal to take sides in a war between other nations or to send supplies, money, or troops to any of the warring parties

objective: a position or goal that an army wants to achieve

occupy: to take control of and install leadership or military rule in another nation by force

pacifist: a person who opposes war, often because of religious or moral beliefs. Many pacifists refuse to serve in active combat.

propaganda: a system of spreading information, ideas, or rumors that support a cause or damage an opposing cause. Posters, advertisements, radio and television broadcasts, films, and other kinds of media can all be used as propaganda.

puppet government: a government controlled by the government of another nation

radar: a detection system that sends out radio signals, which bounce off objects and then return. Radar enables armies to detect objects such as ships or planes above ground or water, regardless of darkness or storms.

refugee: a person who flees his or her home, often during wartime, to escape danger or persecution

reinforcements: additional troops sent in to strengthen, assist, or increase the size of an army

resistance fighters: people in an occupied country who carry out secret operations against the occupying forces

underground: a secret movement of citizens in an occupied country, organized to resist occupying forces

WHO'S WHO?

Winston Churchill (1874–1965)
Born in Oxfordshire, England, Churchill was a descendant of a famous English general, the first Duke of Marlborough. Churchill saw action in Sudan and the Boer War (both in Africa) as an officer and reporter. A member of Great Britain's parliament, he served as first lord of the admiralty (in charge of the British navy) during World War I. Churchill succeeded Neville Chamberlain as prime minister of Great Britain in May 1940. He inspired the British people with his stirring speeches and leadership during the war. He served two terms as prime minister (1940–1945 and 1951–1955).

Dwight David Eisenhower (1890–1969)
Born in Denison, Texas, Eisenhower (nicknamed Ike) graduated from the U.S. Military Academy at West Point, New York, in 1915. He was a career soldier, achieving the rank of colonel by 1939. Eisenhower was quickly selected for promotion, eventually being chosen to command the invasion of North Africa in World War II. His abilities led to his command of the invasion of Sicily and to his supreme command of the invasion of Europe. Eisenhower was elected president of the United States in 1952 and 1956.

Charles de Gaulle (1890–1970)
Charles de Gaulle was born in Lille, France. As an army officer, he pushed for mobile warfare over the trench warfare of World War I. As a colonel, de Gaulle commanded the French 4th Armored Division during the German invasion of France in 1940. Avoiding capture, he made his way to Great Britain, where he organized and led the Free French—a French army of resistance fighters. De Gaulle also was the head of the French government in exile and later became president of France.

Adolf Hitler (1889–1945)
Adolf Hitler was born and raised in Austria. He wanted to study art but failed the entrance exam for the Vienna Academy of Fine Arts. He joined the German infantry in World War I. He distinguished himself in battle and was awarded the Iron Cross First Class for bravery in 1916. After the war, Hitler entered politics. His fiery, outspoken speaking style first got him arrested, then vaulted him to leadership of the Nazi Party and dictatorship of Germany. Faced with defeat by the Allies, Hitler committed suicide on April 30, 1945.

George C. Marshall (1880–1959)
Born in Youngstown Pennsylvania, Marshall graduated from the Virginia Military Institute in 1901. He held a variety of army assignments, wrote about military tactics and strategy, and was regarded as a brilliant officer. In 1939 he became chief of staff of the U.S. Army. He directed the entire army during World War II. He served on the JCS throughout the war. He retired from the army after the war and became U.S. secretary of state, creating the Marshall Plan for the economic recovery of Europe.

General Field Marshal Bernard Law Montgomery (1887–1976)

Born in London, England, Bernard Montgomery had a distinguished military career marked by success and failure. He entered the Royal Military College at Sandhurst, England, in 1907. At the beginning of World War I, he was a lieutenant in the British military. By war's end, he was considered a cunning officer. A general at the onset of World War II and promoted to field marshal in 1944, Montgomery's successes include victory at El Alamein, Egypt, the invasion of Sicily, and the British contributions to D-Day and the Battle of the Bulge. Criticized for poor planning, Montgomery's most notable failure was Operation Market-Garden.

Benito Mussolini (1883–1945)

Born in Dovia, Italy, Benito Mussolini moved to Switzerland as a young man. An outspoken journalist, he was expelled from Switzerland for his ties to the Socialist Party. He was then expelled from the Socialist Party for supporting Italian involvement in World War I. Following World War I, Mussolini established the National Fascist Party, which politically and violently attacked opposing parties. In 1925, Mussolini and his Fascist followers seized control of the Italian government. After the Allied invasion of Italy in 1943, Italian resistance fighters captured and later executed him.

General George S. "Old Blood and Guts" Patton (1885–1945)

George Smith Patton was born in San Gabriel, California. An excellent marksman, Patton later became known for the pearl-handled pistols he carried. His insights into warfare (especially tank warfare) and his fearlessness earned him the nickname Old Blood and Guts. Patton graduated from the Army War College in 1932 and achieved the rank of commanding general in 1941. During World War II, Patton commanded armies in Africa, Italy, and France, where he died in 1945.

Franklin Delano Roosevelt (1882–1945)

Born in Hyde Park, New York, Roosevelt made politics his career. Elected president of the United States in 1932, he started many programs to bring the nation out of the Great Depression. Despite intense political opposition, he backed U.S. military and industrial preparations for entering World War II. He made alliances with Winston Churchill and Joseph Stalin and provided civilian direction to the Joint Chiefs of Staff. His leadership and regular radio addresses inspired the United States to its military and industrial achievements of the war. Roosevelt died in April 1945, before war's end.

Joseph Stalin (1879–1953)

Joseph Stalin was born in Georgia in southwestern Asia. In 1924 he succeeded Vladimir Lenin as head of the Communist Party. He unified the Soviet Union as a dictator, overpowering independent nations and regions and murdering those who opposed him. Great Britain, and later the United States, eventually accepted him as an ally after Germany invaded the Soviet Union. Stalin oversaw Soviet success in the defeat of Germany and went on to set up Communist governments in Eastern Europe.

SOURCE NOTES

4   H. L. Mencken, "H. L. Mencken," *Great Quotations by H. L. Mencken,* 1999, <http://www. cyber-nation.com/victory/ quotations/authors/quotes_mencken_hl.html> (November 2003).

4   Russell Miller, *Nothing Less than Victory: The Oral History of D-Day* (New York: Morrow, 1993), 410.

5   Ibid.

9   William Shirer, *The Rise and Fall of the Third Reich: A History of Nazi Germany* (New York: Fawcett Crest, 1989), 787.

16   "Quotes and Stories," *Sir Winston Churchill,* n.d., <http://www.winstonchurchill.org/ quotes.htm> (April 28, 2003).

29   Franklin Delano Roosevelt, "154 Fireside Chat, White House, Washington, D.C., December 29, 1940," *FDR Fireside Chats,* 2002, <http://www.presidency.ucsb.edu/docs/ fireside/122940.php> (November 2003).

30   Franklin Delano Roosevelt, "Address of the President Delivered by Radio from the White House May 26, 1940, 9:30 P.M., E.S.T.," *FDR Chat 15,* n.d., <http://www.mhric.org/fdr/ chat15.html> (November 2003).

32   "Franklin Delano Roosevelt: Pearl Harbor Address to the Nation," *American Rhetoric,* 2003, <http://www.americanrhetoric.com/ speeches/fdrpearlharbor.htm> (November 2003).

46   Ladislas Farago, *Patton: Ordeal and Triumph* (New York: Dell, 1963), 192.

61   Herbert Stachler, "A Fighter Pilot's Story: 'Lil' Herbie' Stachler," *Quentin C. Aanenson: A Fighter Pilot's Story,* 2003, <http://pages.prodigy.com/ fighterpilot> (November 2003). Used by permission. All rights reserved, Herbert Stachler.

62   Forrest C. Pogue, *The Supreme Command* (Washington, DC: Department of the Army, 1954), 53.

63   Dwight D. Eisenhower, "The Great Crusade," *Eisenhower Overlord Troop Message,* n.d., <http://www.eisenhower.utexas.edu/ssa.htm> (November 2003).

67   Roy Arnn, "Soldiers' Stories: Roy Arnn," *Military.com Remembers D-Day,* 2003, <http:// www.military.com/Content/MoreContent1/ ?file=dday_0043p1> (November 2003). Used by permission. All rights reserved, Roy Arnn and Military.com.

70   B. H. Liddell Hart, *The German Generals Talk* (New York: Morrow, 1979), 245.

71   Paul Carell, *Invasion: They're Coming!* trans. Paul E. Osers (New York: Dutton, 1963), 262.

76   Lou Potter, William Miles, and Nina Rosenblum, *Liberators: Fighting on Two Fronts in World War II* (New York: Harcourt Brace Jovanovich, 1992), 191.

84   Dwight D. Eisenhower, "Dwight D. Eisenhower," *American Experience: The Presidents,* 2003, <http://www.pbs.org/wgbh/ amex/presidents/34_eisenhower/tguide/ eisenhower_iq.html> (November 2003).

SELECTED BIBLIOGRAPHY, FURTHER READING, & WEBSITES

SELECTED BIBLIOGRAPHY

Carell, Paul. *Invasion: They're Coming!* Translated by Paul E. Osers. New York: Dutton, 1963.

Colliers, Larry, and Dominique LaPierre. *Is Paris Burning?* New York: Simon and Schuster, 1965.

Creveld, Martin van. *Supplying War: Logistics from Wallenstein to Patton.* Cambridge, U.K.: Cambridge University Press, 1977.

D'Este, Carlo I. *Patton: A Genius for War.* New York: HarperCollins, 1995.

Dupuy, Trevor N., David L. Bongard, and Richard C. Anderson. *Hitler's Last Gamble: The Battle of the Bulge, December 1944–January 1945.* New York: HarperCollins, 1994.

Fritz, Stephen G. *Frontsoldaten: The German Soldier in World War II.* Lexington, KY: University Press of Kentucky, 1995.

Galland, Adolf. *The First and the Last: The Rise and Fall of the Luftwaffe: 1939–45.* Translated by Mervyn Savill. New York: Ballantine, 1954.

Honey, Maureen. *Creating Rosie the Riveter: Class, Gender and Propaganda during World War II.* Amherst: University of Massachusetts Press, 1984.

James, S. Clayton, and Anna Sharp Wells. *From Pearl Harbor to V-J Day: The American Armed Forces in World War II.* Chicago: Ivan R. Dee, 1995.

Kennett, Lee. *GI: The American Soldier in World War II.* Norman, OK: University of Oklahoma Press, 1997.

Overy, Richard J. *The Air War, 1939–1945.* New York: Stein and Day, 1980.

———. *Why the Allies Won.* New York: W. W. Norton, 1995.

Pyle, Ernie. *Brave Men.* New York: Gosset and Dunlap, 1945.

Ryan, Cornelius. *A Bridge Too Far.* New York: Simon and Schuster, 1974.

———. *The Longest Day.* New York: Simon and Schuster, 1959.

Sherry, Michael S. *The Rise of American Air Power: The Creation of Armageddon.* New Haven, CT: Yale University Press, 1987.

Syrett, David. *The Defeat of the German U-Boats: The Battle of the Atlantic.* Columbia, SC: University of South Carolina Press, 1994.

Toland, John. *The Last 100 Days.* New York: Random House, 1966.

Williams, Vera S. *WACs: Women's Army Corps.* Osceola, WI: Motorbooks International, 1997.

FURTHER READING

Anderson, Christopher J. *The Fall of Fortress Europe: From the Battle of the Bulge to the Crossing of the Rhine.* Broomall, PA: Chelsea House, 2001.

Darby, Jean. *Dwight D. Eisenhower.* Minneapolis: Lerner Publications Company, 2004.

Giblin, James Cross. *The Life and Death of Adolf Hitler.* New York: Clarion, 2002.

Josephson, Judith Pinkerton. *Growing Up in World War II 1941–1945.* Minneapolis: Lerner Publications Company, 2003.

Marx, Trish. *Echoes of World War II.* Minneapolis, Lerner Publications Company, 1994.

McGowen, Tom. *Germany's Lightning War: Panzer Divisions of World War II.* New York: Raintree-Steck Vaughn, 1999.

McKissack, Patricia, and Frederick McKissack. *Red-Tailed Angels: The Story of the Tuskegee Airmen of World War II.* New York: Walker, 2001.

Roberts, Jeremy. *Franklin D. Roosevelt.* Minneapolis: Lerner Publications Company, 2003.

Stassen, Harold, and Marshall Houts. *Eisenhower: Turning the World toward Peace.* Saint Paul: Merrill/Magnus Publishing, 1990.

Whitman, Sylvia. *Uncle Sam Wants You! Military Men and Women of World War II.* Minneapolis: Lerner Publications Company, 1993.

———. *V Is for Victory: The American Home Front during World War II.* Minneapolis: Lerner Publications Company, 1993.

WEBSITES

National D-Day Museum. This museum website offers detailed information on D-Day and the European and Pacific Theaters of Operation, as well as provides resources for students and teachers. <http://www.ddaymuseum.org>

The Perilous Fight: America's World War II in Color. This site features fascinating information on World War II, including the home front, soldiers' experiences, and social aspects of the war. <http://www.pbs.org/perilousfight/>

U.S. Holocaust Memorial Museum. This site provides extensive information on the Holocaust, including survivors' stories, on-line exhibits, an extensive photo and documents library, and resources for students and teachers. <http://www.ushmm.org>

INDEX

ABOUT THE AUTHOR

Margaret J. Goldstein was born in Detroit, Michigan, and attended the University of Michigan. She has edited and written many books for young readers. She lives in Santa Fe, New Mexico.

ACKNOWLEDGMENTS

Thanks to Mr. Herbert "Lil' Herbie" Stachler, who graciously granted permission to print an excerpt from his narrative on his experience at Normandy, page 61, and to Mr. Roy Arnn, whose quotation on page 67 sharing his experience of D-Day appears with the permission of Military.com.

PHOTO ACKNOWLEDGMENTS

The images in this book are used with the permission of: U.S. Coast Guard, pp. 4–5; © Hulton|Archive by Getty Images, pp. 6, 49, 50, 69, 70; United States Holocaust Memorial Museum (USHMM), pp. 7, 8 (courtesy of Estelle Bechoefer), 10 (courtesy of Richard A. Ruppert), 11 (courtesy of Michael O'Hara), 13 (courtesy of Main Commission for the Prosecution of the Crimes against the Polish Nation), 22 (courtesy of National Archives), 26 (courtesy of George Gerzon), 57 (courtesy of KZ-Gedenkstatte Neuengamme), 79 (courtesy of National Archives), 83 (courtesy of Gerald Schwab); National Archives, pp. 12, 15, 16, 18, 37, 39, 40, 42, 44, 47, 54 (top), 58, 68, 73, 74, 76, 80, 90 (second from bottom), 91 (second from bottom); courtesy of the Library of Congress, pp. 14 (LC-USZ62-132602), 20 (LC-USZ62-097396), 23 (LC-USZ62-073335), 25 (LC-USZ62-122640), 27 (LC-USW33-019081), 31 (LC-USE6-D-001276), 33 (LC-USZ62-16555), 35 (top) (LC-SUZ62-102630), 36 (LC-USW33-018434-C), 38 (LC-USZC4-5602), 41 (LC-USZ63-34571), 43 (LC-USW33-026191-C), 46 (LC-USZ62-084988), 48 (LC-USZ62-070812), 51 (LC-USZ62-098984), 52 (LC-USZ62-129782), 54 (bottom) (LC-USE6-D-007781), 56 (LC-USZ62-080531), 63 (LC-USZ62-079090), 78 (LC-USZ62-099268), 90 (top) (LC-USW3-019093-C), 90 (second from top) (LC-USZ62-00918), 90 (center) (LC-USZ62-096046), 90 (bottom) (LC-USZ62-103399), 91 (second from top) (LC-USZ62-88713), 91 (bottom) (LC-USW33-019081); Laura Westlund, pp. 17, 21, 24, 66, 77, 81, 87; © Bettmann/CORBIS, pp. 28, 34, 67; U.S. Office of War information, courtesy of the Franklin D. Roosevelt Library, p. 29; © CORBIS, pp. 35, 75; © Hulton-Deutsch Collection/CORBIS, pp. 45, 82, 84; © Jeff Albertson/CORBIS, p. 53; © Museum of Flight/CORBIS, p. 55 (top); Minneapolis Public Library, Kittleson World War II Collection, p. 55 (bottom); Smithsonian Institution, p. 60; Dwight D. Eisenhower Library, pp. 62, 91 (center); © The Mariners' Museum/CORBIS, p. 65; Franklin D. Roosevelt Library, p. 71; American Red Cross, p. 72; *Illustrated London News,* Royalty Free, p. 91 (top).

Cover: © Bettmann/CORBIS.